Beyond Vatican II

The Church at a New Crossroads

Beyond Vatican II

The Church at a New Crossroads

Rev. Claude Barthe

Translated by Deborah B. Cole

Roman Catholic Books

P. O. Box 2286 • Fort Collins, CO 80522

BooksforCatholics.com

ISBN 1-929291-83-3

Printed in the U.S.A.

This book is based especially on material from accounts and analyses of the contemporary life of the Church, substantially reworked and augmented, which have appeared in the quarterly review, *Catholica*.

*"And behold an Angel of the Lord stood by him:
and a light shined in the room: and he striking Peter
on the side, raised him up, saying: Arise quickly.
And the chains fell off from his hands."*

(Acts of the Apostles, 12:7)

Table of Contents

INTRODUCTION

...A time to rebuild

1965-2005: Forty years. Forty years have elapsed since the close of the Second Vatican Council. During this period, many things have changed for the Church and for the world. The extent of the transformation poses a kind of paradox for Catholics: this Council, which had promised to usher in a new era in the relations between religion and society, has instead greatly advanced their decoupling, officially or unofficially sanctioning the total autonomy of the latter. In its wake, Catholics became defined as "for" or "against" the Council, with nuances, degrees, or shifts along the spectrum of agreement and dissent. For or against the Council? Today, the devastating power of ultra-modernity has completely changed the way in which the question is to be posed and answered.

Henceforward, the fundamental reality for the Church, at least in France and the West, is its effacement, not merely social but psychological. Although anecdotal, it is significant that photos of Vatican II gatherings, which have been ceaselessly reproduced without the need for elaboration as representing a revolution in the Church, today strike the average reader as the triumphalist clericalism of another age. On balance, the Church

Herself appears to have become insignificant. And yet, interior divisions persist. Is it not therefore urgent that Catholics of good will join together to seek a solution? Unless, of course, it is already too late.

It is clear that today's Catholics are engaged in an undertaking that is utterly overwhelming and is only one of innumerable dramatic episodes in the history of the Church. The present episode is not the most negligible, if we consider the immense damage to souls — from a human perspective, the greatest hemorrhage that has ever been produced — but it is also among the most mediocre. The tragedy lies precisely in the fact that we have the abysmal reduction of nearly everyone and everything to mediocrity. And yet this story, our story, remains that of salvation, directed entirely by the Lord who, in the end times, will appear in an instant like a flash of lightning which will rend the veil of the celestial sanctuary from east to west. For all that, the story remains at once human and divine, that is to say a story of saints and sinners among whose principal ranks are the shepherds.

For these pastors, the sense of the marginalization of Catholicism and its consequences within the Church has become an obsession. The French bishops talk about little else in their conversations, in their speeches, during their Paris meetings, their gatherings at Lourdes or their ad limina visits to Rome: the figures for children being catechized or the number of priests remaining in their dioceses. It is well known that after the Council, Sunday worship diminished considerably and its constituents grew much older: it melted by two-thirds or three-quarters. Yet even today, the meltdown is continuing. This is true except for well preserved urban parishes or other places served by new communities or traditionalists from different backgrounds. But this phenomenon of selectivity, choosing one's church according to one's sensibility, has contributed to sapping the vital energy of ordinary parishes, all the while reinforcing the closed character of the pastorate of privileged locales. In order to survive, the Catholicism of this time of Great Apostasy is organized in networks. Make no mistake: it is a matter of survival.

More troubling yet for the future of the Faith is the collapse of the number of catechized children in the past decade. Formerly, catechesis had involved almost the whole population, even the non-practicing. Until around 1980, quite a few children still underwent catechesis. Today, the courses of instruction in the Faith are deserted. Those who do attend are often the little modern "barbarians" who no longer have the benefit of the Christian presuppositions in which even the non-practicing had lived in earlier times. Young people increasingly enter into marriage without ever having been catechized.

It is true that catechesis today also commonly applies to adults who desire baptism or who although baptized rediscover their faith like beginners. That could hold certain comfort. Unfortunately, the level of perseverance of these adults, especially the newly baptized, is low. As for the content of the instruction, it is often worse than deficient. Bluntly, the normal transmission of the Catholic faith is no longer assured. A weakening has occurred in the very foundations of the instruction. There is no doubt that something went wrong in the renewal of Vatican II.

The decline in the numbers of priests becomes more serious because of the following vicious circle: whatever the good will of the laypersons who maintain religious instruction, without priest-educators, the number of children with religious formation will fall; and if children are either not catechized or poorly catechized, there will be no more vocations.

The figures for the collapse of the priesthood are well known: after the Council, vocations plunged precipitously, a sign that a profound fissure was opening. Then in the 1980s, they stabilized, so that annual ordinations of diocesan priests in

France have been maintained at the impoverished level of 120 or 130. This was a mere lull; the curve once again begins to descend, and in 2003, only 105 diocesan priests were ordained in France. More than half of French dioceses had no ordination this year, so that in the aggregate priests have declined by 700 to 800 a year. What is more, the decline in the number of seminarians has resumed (1163 in 1993, 831 in 2002). Until now, vocations were still numerous in certain relatively flourishing communities or seminaries tacitly or expressly rejecting "the spirit of the Council" or else trying to place themselves outside it. Today, even if the new communities and the various traditionalist movements remain as reservoirs for vocations, a decline must inevitably be felt there as well.

Taking into account the number and the average age of the diocesan clergy in France, which is about to pass seventy, and the number of "departures," which exceeds fifteen percent a year and henceforth will involve a significant proportion of young priests, within roughly ten years, a number of French dioceses will no longer have active priests. Certain people rejoice at this prospect, on the grounds that the more "identity-minded" young priests will soon constitute the great majority. But they will resemble missionaries dispersed across a religious desert. Forty years after Vatican II, in the majority of Western nations, society is witnessing the death of the priesthood and the disappearance of visible Catholicism.

It is clear that the Council is not the only responsible party. Not even a Council energized by the events of May 1968 in France. No one, however, can deny that the social crisis, in the form of a paroxysm of individualism that assaults all institutions, all groups, and all tendencies, would never have been what it has been without Vatican II, as the event ultimately unfolded. Whatever the responsibility — direction taken forty years ago or reorientation since then — the most obvious fruits are there to be seen: disappearance of the priesthood and massive religious ignorance. In fact, the evil is not that Vatican II took place, but rather the opposite: no one, I think, denies that a reform of the Church was highly necessary during the 1960s. But to put it simply, there was a foundation of rock, which it was certainly necessary to "clean" and recover by means of a true reform; instead, it has been replaced by a foundation of sand.

I will surely be reproached for excessive criticism of Vatican II, directly or indirectly, in the course of these pages; especially for not taking sufficiently into account the bad interpretations of the Council. I would respond that after forty years of bad interpretation, it is high time that the "good interpretation" emerge and establish itself in order to eliminate once and for all the "bad." And this is not just words; I am, indeed, a supporter of an interpretation of Vatican II, good by definition, if it is that of the Magisterium. And it is even, finally, the purpose of these pages. Perhaps the time has come when all Catholics of good will may finally be able to unite in soliciting and bringing about an interpretation of the full meaning of Vatican II.

PART I

TAKING STOCK

CHAPTER I

A straightforward look

Vatican II deliberately chose to break the mold in its basic goal as well as in its authority. This, according to some, is its great virtue; according to others, its essential flaw. Content and authority are like the two poles of the magisterial function of the Church. The content of Church teaching as such is greater precision, based on various possible connections, brought to the Deposit of Faith. As for its authority, it is that of the Pope alone or of the Pope together with the bishops. They carry out their full responsibility as successors of Peter and of the Apostles by calling for the full assent of the faithful to what they teach. Everything transmitted in this manner demands belief; conversely, nothing is required to be believed by the faithful without it being part of the magisterial teaching.

In ecumenical councils which have instituted reform initiatives, legislative ordinances, and sometimes decrees issued in union with separated churches, there are always retained as an essential certain doctrinal teachings that are elaborated in their formal assemblies. Indeed, the gathering of the shepherds of the Church is above all the most expressive organ of the "living Magisterium" or more broadly, the Church's "living tradition."[1] Ever since Nicea, when bishops representing the entire world assemble, it is in order to amplify the voice of the Good Shepherd enunciating that Truth which is necessary for salvation.

Below the dogma

Now, as much in its essence as in its form, Vatican II chose a different option. In its doctrinal work, three texts can be considered definitive, revealing points of view that were frankly new, relative to the existing dogmatic corpus. These were the result of a project carried out by the Secretary of the Pontifical Council for Promoting Christian Unity that was broken down into three outlines: the decree *Unitatis Redintegratio*, on ecumenism; the declaration *Nostra Aetate*, on relations of the Church with non-Christian religions; and the declaration *Dignitatis Humanae*. This project had a unique ecumenical goal.

From the point of view of doctrine, the Council wanted to innovate by introducing a certain sense of legitimacy in the diversity of beliefs. In itself, this character of *innovation* is a good thing. It is useful to recall in this regard the famous response made to the question, "Is Christian doctrine, then, not open to any progress in the Church of Christ?" St. Vincent de Lérins replied, "Of course it is necessary that it be, and plenty of it! [...] But always with this reservation, that this progress constitute truly progress and not alteration: the characteristic of progress being that each thing grows while remaining itself; the characteristic of alteration being that one thing is transformed into another."[2] The dogmatic teaching of the Church has, in effect, an *innovative* aspect in the understanding of the Deposit of Faith. The teachings of the Church, notably those of the councils, are acts which strictly speaking do not innovate since they retain the contents of the Apostolic tradition. However, each time they are pronounced, these judgments bring something new in terms of precision, taking into account circumstances of the historical moment.

The ultimate teaching authority was lacking in Vatican II: "only pastoral," that is to say, without dogmatic authority, the last Council saw itself in some way as a non-council. The atypical principle of this Council, affirmed so many times afterward, was posited the first day, Thursday, October 11, 1962, by the famous opening statement of Pope John XXIII, *Gaudet Mater*

Ecclesia. Vatican II, distinguishing itself from all the councils of the past, would dogmatize neither in the positive sense (canons) nor in the negative sense (anathemas). On the one hand, there being universal assent to the doctrine "which had been transmitted with the precision of terms and concepts which was the particular glory of the Council of Trent and of the First Vatican Council," it was now only a matter of presenting it in the manner "that meets the needs of the present day" and giving it "the forms and proportions of a magisterium which is predominantly pastoral in character;" on the other hand, the Church of today preferred to "make use of the medicine of mercy rather than that of severity," and so She judged that rather than condemning, She would do better to respond "to the needs of the present day by demonstrating the validity of her teaching." Furthermore, Pope John XXIII announced that Vatican II would not be antimodern: "In the present social situation, [the prophets of doom] see only ruin and calamity. [...] It seems necessary to Us to express Our complete disagreement with these prophets of doom who are always predicting catastrophes, as if the end of the world were imminent."

When the Magisterium involves itself, it can only do so totally. Yet here it only did so by halves. The motives for this strange *via media* were complex. On the part of the conciliar majority, it was a matter of creating more doctrinal "openness," without contradicting previous doctrine. But the minority, overwhelmed during the first days of the gathering, quickly came to emphasize the absence of infallible authority of the texts, which, according to the minority, relativized their scope.

It is possible, in fact, to talk about the lack of clearly delimited content even before speaking about the absence of authority. This is particularly true of the decree on ecumenism, *Unitatis Redintegratio*, which failed to state the objective being pursued in characterizing the sought-for unity. In order for there to be a Catholic ecumenism that is neither a development of the traditional "unionism" (with the *return* of the separated churches) nor a heterodox drift (a march toward a kind of federal Church which would contain the confessions of all the reunited Christians), there had to be a "pastoral" third way. After having proposed, "By ecumenism are meant all the contemporary efforts to realize ecumenism," the sub-commission charged with the matter dropped all pretenses of a definition.

Whatever the confusion, this teaching was strictly speaking innovative: in effect, not only was the Magisterium of the Church never enlisted in this direction, but everything indicated that it was engaged in the contrary direction. Thus, where traditional teaching affirmed the necessity of belonging to the Church, in reality or by desire, in order to be saved, *Unitatis Redintegratio*, n. 3 spoke of "the significance and importance in the mystery of salvation" of separated churches and communities as such. While the previous teaching spoke of possible "tolerance" of error in religious matters, *Dignitatis Humanae,* n. 2 lauds a "liberty" — in the sense of "public liberty," i.e. a right— "that in religious matters, no one is to be forced to act in a manner contrary to his own beliefs, whether privately or publicly." As a principle of dialogue with other religions, the aforementioned teaching spoke of the unicity of the paths to salvation, and *Nostra Aetate*, n. 2 desired that the Church accord a "sincere reverence" (*observantia:* religious respect) to other "ways," to wit to non-Christian religions as such, by virtue of the positive elements they could contain. Like it or not, it is impossible to avoid the conclusion — emphasized by the extremists of the interreligious and ecumenical dialogue — that to recognize a certain legitimacy in the diversity of beliefs implies that God wishes, that is, does not condemn, this religious pluralism. It implies that God desires and does not condemn a diversity of Christian confessions. Thus, Vatican II accomplished a sure opening to the modern *Weltanschauung,* in alignment with the Pope John XXIII's mission in convoking it. It did so as much in the content of its teaching, that is, by a certain number of guarantees given to pluralism and thus relativism, as in the non-dogmatic manner in which the teaching was delivered.

Certainly, these elements must not obscure the fact that the whole of the corpus of the last Council contains very beautiful passages, notable advances and precisions (on the foundations of the sacramentality of the episcopacy, on the conditions of the exercise of the ordinary Magisterium), weighty documents like the decree *Ad Gentes*, and on the missions. It is true that other documents, like the Constitution *Gaudium et Spes*, are oriented in the same direction of "opening" as the texts that one could characterize broadly as ecumenical. On balance, it seems as though everything is tending toward the search for a "third way" in the Council. The most "open" texts are moderated by traditional statements, and the classical statements are strewn with caveats allowing them to be neutralized ("The use of the Latin language is to be preserved in the Latin rites. But since...," *Sacrosanctum Conciliu*, n. 36).

Waiting for interpretation

Vatican II did indeed exert an influence calculated to move the whole Church in new directions. This is the Gordian knot: it was a non-council patterned on a council, or rather in place of a council. The intangible but undeniable involvement of the Pope and the bishops in new doctrinal matters — while not formally defining anything — left a *de facto* doctrinal construct. Applying the principle that revolutions impede true reforms, it could be argued that the innovation of Vatican II obstructed the magisterial process: under the appearance of renovation, it prevented the progressive and vital development that might have been hoped for (and whose elements, which have nothing to do with the "spirit of the Council," are moreover found in a good number of its documents.)

As a consequence, we find ourselves today in uncharted

waters, in a state of magisterial weightlessness. Since Vatican II, it appears that the Magisterium, which as such defines and decides in the ultimate sense, no longer wishes to carry out that role.[3] It is a very modern situation, in which the non-law (here, essentially a doctrinal non-law) plays the role of and takes the place of the law. In other words, it is an ideological system in the style of a meta-discourse that impregnates the whole of ecclesial life. It is true that the situation is far from tyrannical, given a weakened institution whose personnel are riddled with doubts. It is the case, though, that in practical terms, the various "ecumenical" texts of which I have spoken bind the entire life of the Church.

Supporting the preceding analysis is one massive fact: the Magisterium no longer assumes the proper role of the classical Magisterium, to wit, the *interpretation* of the Deposit of Faith and of the prior Magisterium. The endless debates about the "good interpretation" of Vatican II have demonstrated the multitude of possible readings, each claiming to be the "good interpretation." These would emphasize, if such were needed, that the tension between practically contradictory readings is part of the Council's "pastoral" character. Indeed, this Council must be interpreted, not only as every text must be in order to be understood, but because it did not bequeath to itself the capacity to be explicated, namely the ultimate authority of teaching in the name of Christ.

Everything being equal, one could say as much concerning the new liturgy, which no longer has the ritual framework corresponding in worship to the dogmatic framework in teaching. The liturgy of Pope Paul VI, like the Council and for analogous reasons, also requires interpretation. And we know how diverse are the interpretations in that arena.[4] The famous saying of *lex orandi, lex credendi* is applicable to the relations that exist between the respective contents of the conciliar teaching and of the liturgical reform ("opening" to the world, immanentizing of the liturgy in the reform of Pope Paul VI). In the same way that the teaching of Vatican II is not expressed as a *law* of the Faith, the development of worship under Vatican II lacks the character of a *law* of prayer.

This new liturgy, and most especially the new Mass, is indeed the concrete, palpable translation of the spirit of the Council. Its characteristics are analogous to those of the Council. From the point of view of content, that which could offend modern ears has been erased (until the latest edition of the missal of Pope Paul VI, in 2003, the word "soul" had disappeared from the prayers for the dead). There is troubling slippage in the liturgical message as such (one thinks, for example, about the turning of the altar "toward the people" and considers what it represents as a modification of its sacred meaning; or else the suppression of the sacrificial offering). And, as I have said, the character of the liturgical *law* is profoundly attenuated (infinite multiplicity of possible variants, diminution of the concept of hierarchical priesthood).

Now the new Mass is concretely the means by which the Council has permeated the ranks of the Christian people. This includes the manner of its transmission: the Mass of Pope Paul VI transmits accurately, especially when its avoids excesses, the essence of Vatican II, namely the installation of a bourgeois ideology into the Church, in the sense of liberalism, and in the aesthetic sense of the lifestyle and thought of the end of the 20th century and the beginning of the 21st.

It is hardly necessary to repeat yet again that for all who have eyes to see, the new liturgy, compared with the traditional liturgy and what remains of the Eastern rites, is a desacralized liturgy, a "profane" liturgy, that is to say a liturgy whose profane style and mode of thought have impeded access to the transcendent. Is it necessary to repeat that this has resulted in immense spiritual damage, not only to faithful Catholics but also to a whole civilization?

The liturgical damage is but a sign. Without undertaking an exhaustive analysis, I would like to single out two aspects of the considerably worse evil that the Church would need to remedy today, even if all the preceding analysis were without merit: the disintegration of the *Credo* and the democratization of the divine constitution of the Church.

CHAPTER II

To each his own Credo

When speaking of the privatizing of faith, it is important to avoid obfuscation by undue comparisons with that of the sixteenth century. While the present phenomenon of the *un-dogmatizing* of Catholicism certainly has its connections with the demands of free inquiry, it is actually much more in line with the *Social Contract*. With regard to "He who hears you hears me," Luke 10:16, Luther merely modified the function of communicating Revelation in its integrity from the Pope and the bishops to each baptized individual reading Scripture under the inspiration of the Holy Spirit. The claim of independence peculiar to modernity certainly owes much to this development, but it is more radical, in the sense that reason, starting out with Kant in its infancy, tends toward autonomy not only in reading the content of the Word of God, but even more in constructing it concretely. The function of *interpretation* of Revelation, then, changes not only its subject but its meaning.

What's more, it is a matter that is hardly necessary to describe. One can simply point to "surveys on the faith of the French," more remarkable for the fact that they result from the assumption that it is perfectly normal for Catholics to have critical judgments concerning the *Credo* than for the disastrous results that they serenely reveal: twenty percent of practicing Catholics believe only "a little" in the Resurrection of Christ; fourteen percent believe only "a little" in his divinity, etc.

The claims of freedom

The theme of subjectivism, so dear to sociologists of religion, is of the same type. A Catholic who turns his back on hell while embracing reincarnation does so without any reference to authority, unlike the Protestant, who in submission to the principle of *sola scriptura*, adopts a vegetarian diet in supposed fidelity to a verse of Genesis. The legitimizing of subjectivism in faith is really a modern form of hedonism, what mystical writers call "spiritual gluttony;" the criterion for belief becomes its power to give the believer pleasure and a sense of expansion. After all, isn't the purpose of religion to temper the "tragic" character of the human condition?

The *sensus fidelium*, invoked by dissenting theologians who are hardly ever read today but who have wielded devastating influence, is conjoined to individualized dogma and is thus transformed into an authoritative *consensus*; this subsumes moral teaching. *Consensus* becomes authority because nature abhors a vacuum, and society, even the thoroughly democratized Catholic ecclesiastic society of today, aspires to a unifying principle. It is to be found in the voice of the majority (the "dynamic" majority, or in Marc Sangnier's words, the "adult" majority) of the people of God. The freedom to use artificial contraception or the possibility of the ordination of women thus become the products of evolving society and the rising consciousness of Christians.[5]

Subjectivity becomes an ideological absolute which constrains any counterclaims. Theologians and pastors exercise the right of "diversity" at the same time as they deny the right of any opposition to it. It is notable, for example, that priests who are opposed to the repeated reminders of Rome concerning the inadmissibility of serving Communion to "remarried" individuals brook no opposition and even insist on their right to bless such unions. In contrast, priests — often young — who consider that such people must not be admitted to Communion run up against the intense hostility of their colleagues and parish councils, to the point of being ostracized or removed from their positions. Here is the classic pattern in which those who claim the freedom to disobey utterly deny the freedom to obey.

Without reiterating what I explained in the previous chapter, I must point out that the Magisterium that resulted from Vatican II did so to speak integrate this autonomization of the interpretation of Revelation by directly suspending the dogmatic function in its strict sense.[6] We only note here the paradoxical authoritarian aspect that the teaching function acquires, an appearance only since the reality is a generalized revolt.

The members of the hierarchy have noted that teaching which binds or looses for eternity has become incomprehensible for our epoch, attached as it is to individual freedom as a founding principle, liberty that prohibits the very notion of irrevocability. But since they try all the same to obtain adherence in doctrinal questions, they can only do so in the name of disciplinary obedience and no longer in the name of obedience to the Faith. As a result, there has been a substantial extension of what is considered the authentic Magisterium, the most eminent of the non-infallible teachings, but which, from this very fact, cannot be imposed as doctrine which binds consciences irrevocably.

The most flagrant case, clearly, is that of the doctrine contained in *Humanae Vitae*, which without ever having been designated as relating to the adherence of faith (applying itself in this case to an appeal to natural law), has nevertheless been made the object, especially under the pontificate of John Paul II, of increasing appeals to its obligation. This objective authoritarianism merely reinforces subjective disobedience, which is based on the judgment rendered ultimately by the consciences of the spouses.

Now, the very nature of what is in question in this example underlines the impasse involved in the use of the simply authentic Magisterium. More than in a doctrinal question, in a matter of natural morality, the designation of the degree of authority corresponds to the degree of obligation. If the proposition of n. 14 of *Humanae Vitae*[7] were not irrevocable, it would not be able to impose an absolute moral authority; if it were not irrevocable, indeed it would not be a matter of the law inscribed in the heart. Conversely, if there is fault in not applying it, it is because it must be received absolutely as true, everywhere and forever. The third path, that of the simple authentic Magisterium, would say that the non-accomplishment of a provisional — revocable — moral precept would, despite everything, be a sin. Which is absurd.

One could point to the liturgical field to show the intersection of the "laissez-faire," let-it-go attitude which has become like a new principle of liturgical regulation, and its application in parishes, which turns anarchy into a principle. So we see a double loss. On the otherwise laudable grounds that the public worship of the Church must "fulfill the community," what we see is that ritualism, sacred language deemed to be incomprehensible, the mystery of symbols, the entire chain of traditional memory, all have been banished with the wave of a hand. The result is not only the explosion of a "multi-community" but the self-celebration of the community by means of a rite as personalized as possible. The other aspect of liturgical privatization, even worse in a sense, is the fact that the *reaction* against this post-Vatican II rite usually takes the form of a demand for privatization, that each be allowed to practice the liturgy that suits his sensibility. Danièle Hervieu-Léger is right to say that the circle of modernity encloses even anti-modern demands. This, it should be noted, is because of the ease of using this type of argument to make oneself heard.

Pastors on the sidelines

The preceding example of *Humanae Vitae* demonstrates the ambiguity of privatizing the regulatory function of faith.

Certainly it is clear that the authoritarian drift, loudly and hypocritically denounced by all of the dissenting theology, especially in the moral domain, has no chance of going beyond what it has become — a discourse without practical force. The claims of conscience, on the other hand, have the means to impose themselves by a tyranny of opinion via the usual channels which function in modern democracies, notably the media.

Speaking more generally, the privatization of faith is surely one of the most sensitive points of encounter with the new authoritarian tendencies of democracy. Sociological studies of the religious phenomenon eagerly mark a division between those religions which accept and those which reject debate, between those that conform to democratic values and those which cannot be reconciled with them. Certain sociologists of religion are disturbed by the fact that one can actually apply to a Benedictine monastary the treatment reserved for sects that threaten individual liberty by pointing to the guru-like power exercised by the superior, the alienation represented by the practice of obedience and goods in common, not to mention perpetual vows, etc. It is not implausible that a chokehold could be placed on the claim that individual consciences can be bound by a transcendent authority; in a multitude of such conflicts, the courts could sustain the claim that such constraints are contrary to the rights universally recognized by democracies.

This evocation of the latent collision between modern society and the essence of Catholicism — since it touches upon one of the aspects of the Lordship of Christ — brings us back to the internal crisis. Evasion and immobility once more confirm the privatizing of faith.

You will remember that in 1998 a new "working edition" of the *Jerusalem Bible* was published with notes interpreting certain passages of the New Testament as denying the divinity of Christ, without being denounced in any way by the pastors of the Church. Was this not, in effect, an endorsement of the subjectivizaton of the *Credo*? I take this example deliberately, as much because it concerns the pivot of the Christian faith, the divinity of Christ, as because it results from the modernist interpretation of dogma; since these notes reaffirm that the New Testament contradicts itself: it usually attests that Jesus Christ is God, but also sometimes that He is not. In the mind of the author of the notes, Fr. Boismard, this presents no problem, since the very notion of the divinity of Christ can be interpreted diversely according to the context and, even more radically, the notion of the definition of what must be believed is susceptible to relativistic evaluation. (At the time of Le Roy and Loisy, one spoke of "symbolism," and today we practice "hermeneutics.")

In reality, if there is a legitimate context for the comprehension of the Word of God, it is that which takes account of the obstacles it has found historically in the erroneous interpretations usually linked to philosophical concepts or predetermined systems of thought — in other words, of private interpretations diverging from the public interpretation. The denunciation of these deviant interpretations was integrated into the *Credo* (the symbol of Nicea to avert the theses of Arius). Today, we find ourselves at a point where the very objectivity of the announcement of the message is dissolved in the subjectivity of interpretation.

CHAPTER III

Integration of the democratic model

"Since 1789," wrote Bernanos, "it seems that She [the Church] has abandoned the hope of reconquering the lost world. [...] Her ambition thereafter has been limited to withdrawing, after a fashion, to the place where the wounding pity of the conquerors permits Her to be outside the walls of the town, in the manner prescribed by the Mosaic law for impure women and snake charmers. She boasts, on the contrary, of having recovered what She laughably calls Her liberty."[8]

Identity crisis

To deal with the crisis of authority in the Church after referring to the atomization of the *Credo* is to deal with Her identity crisis, not in a banal or superficial sense, but in the metaphysical sense of self-comprehension of Her very being. At the root of this crisis of authority is doubt on the part of the men of the Church about their intrinsic character as *prophets*, as spokesmen, as bearers of the unique Word, confronted as they are by the modern response to the legitimacy of that Word: voices, *voces*, diverse and multiple, in place of *the* Voice. If they themselves have not installed them, pastors have allowed the installation of forums in place of thrones of unique truth.

The whole history of Catholic liberalism (and in a way, the history of anti-liberalism) can be summed up in this: a progressive destabilization caused by the subversion of the principle of the authority of the Bride of Christ in the name of the principle of liberty of conscience. A century ago, in his Letter *Testem Benevolentiae* (1899), Leo XIII condemned those who "hold such liberty should be allowed in the Church, that her supervision and watchfulness being in some sense lessened, allowance be granted the faithful, each one to follow out more freely the leading of his own mind and the trend of his own proper activity. They are of opinion that such liberty has its counterpart in the newly given civil freedom which is now the right and the foundation of almost every secular state." From that point, as we know, we have come to a situation of placid emancipation from ecclesial guardianship. The most normative documents are openly challenged not only by the faithful but by priests and teachers, with tacit and sometimes active endorsement of a notable part of the episcopate. In the great majority, as I have said, Catholics feel themselves completely free to reconstitute their *Credo* and their morality. A systematic downward pressure results in the assumption that every authoritative document is open to debate and invites discussion.

In all this, however, the crucial point for the past two hundred years is that which Bernanos illuminates, namely the complicity of the spokesmen, the men of the Church, with liberalism — in this particular case with its aspect of doctrinal free exchange of ideas — a much more serious collusion than that with communism which the late Cardinal Decourtray denounced in latter times.

The modern response of pastoral authority exercised in the name of Christ has thus been interiorized. At first this was done practically, *politically,* rather than theoretically.[9] Then, from Vatican II on, theorizing occurred surrounding common law. From *Dignitatis Humanae*, which requested of the supposedly neutral State rights and liberties for "religious groups" (n. 4), to the famous Dagens report, which specified that "today, in their great majority, French Catholics consider themselves as citizens with full rights" and that they "unabashedly admit the seculari-

ty of the State,"[10] we have seen pastors accept democratic operation in principle, the effect of which is to make their role as
teaching successors to the Apostles a mere afterthought.[11]

The practice of rallying to what Pope Leo XIII termed the
"new right" thus became theory, and the theory reinforced practice. Here is a pointed example, by no means trivial: the
Church at one time took it as a judicial assault that every religious marriage had to be proceeded by a civil marriage, and
denounced as a "non-law" the civil regulation of divorce
(divorce was not tolerated except in the case where the ecclesiastic tribunal had already pronounced the nullity of the marriage); today, in France, the episcopal judges, that is, the diocesan ecclesiastic tribunals, do not agree to begin an action of nullity of marriage before a civil divorce has been granted.

And this is powerfully revealing: in the heart of democratic
society, a group or an association may not adopt rules of internal
functioning except in the measure that such rules do not contra-
vene the general rules of the Social Contract — at least in principle, but with a restrained application to the Church until recently.

If they deviate from this norm (for example, all the requirements of monastic life or more generally submission to magisterial hierarchy), they will be admitted by the modern State only
on sufferance and reduced little by little by an ever-expanding
conception of public order. For the democratic State, these
internal non-democratic regulations are respected only to the
extent that they are freely adopted by their members; but it is
understood that the latter can dispense with them at any
moment, normally by leaving the religious group to which they
belong, without their congregation, parish, or diocese being
able to punish them; but also, more and more frequently, calling these religious entities to judicial or legal arbitration with
secular institutions. And this pattern will gain momentum as,
for example, there are demands for damages by members of a
religious order who leave it on the grounds of "moral abuse"

which they were forced to undergo during their year of novitiate where their correspondence was controlled, penances were imposed, etc.

We are thus confronted with Church authorities pretending to accept as "neutral" a social system founded on Rousseauian principles. And this contamination occurs before our eyes, without a single direct objection on the part of those accountable. Ecclesiastic society in this way has, little by little, integrated — with, it is true, zones of resistance, reactions at the foot and at the summit, delays — a mode of authority other than its own. The sociologist Jean-Paul Willaime has noted the homogenization of Protestantism and Catholicism, in the following form: there is a "Protestantization" of individual religious attitudes and a "Catholicization " of ecclesiastical organizations; the two terms — and this is very important in its demonstration — being taken in a secular sense and not in the sense of conversion of one into the other.[12] By Protestant secularizing, he means that individual behaviors, Catholic as well as Protestant, including in the milieux most strongly identified with each, are marked "by individualization, criticism of teaching authority, declericalization, the desire for a greater democratization of church life." By Catholic secularizing, he understands that the responsible clerics, including Protestants, tend to become similar to figures in political life or modern enterprise. They have to manage and federate an internal diversity that is ever greater; their functions tend to become specialized; and a very great importance is attached to their charism (to remain within sociological jargon, the "structure" henceforth being replaced by "enthusiasm.") In other words, there is a symbiosis of the mode of government and mode of obedience in the churches, and especially in the Catholic Church, with those of modern societies.

Federating instead of uniting

What constitutes the matter on which the apostolic authority acts is the confession of faith of each of the baptized, in words and acts. If, then, the ecclesiastic authority has noticeably distanced itself from this matter, it ceases, *de facto* (I say *de facto* to denote the violence of the fact) to represent an instrument of unity, at least of unity in the classic sense, and becomes, on the contrary — always *de facto* — the administrator of diversity. In this way, most gravely and most obviously, the modification of individual behavior and mode of government provokes a crisis in the unity of faith. Or to put it in a nutshell: the role of authority vis-à-vis the Faith would henceforth be to *federate* and no longer to *unite*.

It would require volumes and libraries to review the public doctrinal errors asserted by pastors, theologians, professors, and Christian groups of all kinds. What is most serious is that the free expression of heterodoxy has become like a fundamental liberty which cannot be reversed. The gravest dissents regarding dogma and morals are today expressed peaceably, and above all casually. In any case, for thirty-five years, no sentence of exclusion for heresy has been pronounced by the episcopal or Roman hierarchy, except rare or marginal cases. At the very best, there has been a "notification" of errors, as was the case for example of Fr. Vidal, a Redemptorist, regarding moral heresies, and Fr. Dupuis, a Jesuit, regarding heresies about Christ and the Church as unique means of salvation.

But after all, one could say that there have been periods of roiling error, which, if not as serious, at least were very dramatic. The drama here is that today schism remains latent, diversity does not explode: the faithful, the preachers, the cardinals can hold divergent professions on points of faith or morals formerly considered as fundamental (the indissolubility of marriage, for example), all the while each and every one continuing to be considered Catholic. To borrow a concept beloved of theologians of religion, the label of "Catholic" has become ever more inclusive.

Thus the democratic modality of authority serves as reference, establishing the lines of force like a magnet. More precisely, external ecumenism serves as a mold for the new way of confessing the Faith. Cardinal Kasper, president of the Pontifical Council for Promoting Christian Unity, said precisely in this regard: "We understand ecumenism today no longer in the sense of return, in which others must 'convert' and become 'Catholic.' This was expressly abandoned by Vatican II. [...] Each Church has its riches and its gifts of the Spirit, and it is a question of exchanging them, and not that we have to become 'Protestants' or they 'Catholics' in the sense of the confessional form of Catholicism."[13]

The external consequences of such a principle of "unity" are evidently disastrous for the mission of the Church, but even more disastrous are the internal consequences, because such an approach has as its first effect the modification of what one could call the ecclesial being of Catholics (the Faith, the sense of communion) and not that of separated Christians. This means that at least in principle — and even if reality resists it — a federating authority of diversity in faith tends to replace the regulating authority of a unity in the Faith.

Rather than consider the frittering away of the *Credo* into relativism, as I have done in the last chapter, at bottom it is much more instructive to look at how this diversity holds together. It becomes clear that the ancient matrix of *regula fidei* has tended to be replaced by an ecumenical matrix, that we might characterize as federal, that is to say the demand for pluralism within unity. And besides, if the latent schism some day becomes declared, it will not so much relate to the fragmentation of the *Credo,* like the old schisms; it will relate more radically to the demand for a pluralistic Church. There will not be a schism, for example, between people who believe that Christ is God and people who do not believe it, but rather between those who believe that one cannot be Catholic while denying the divinity of Christ and those who believe one can be Catholic in denying it as well as affirming it. In other words, sooner or later there will be a clarification of this type: the separation between an ecumenical Catholic Church and a Catholic Church without any other qualifier.

We could study this phenomenon under very different aspects. One of these, the forum, which represents the organized coexistence of different opinions, transmits this osmosis well, at all levels of ecclesiastic life, although with a certain delay between the functioning of democratic society and the internal functioning of the Church. It is a matter of the mechanism governing opinion being applied to an otherwise very traditional mode in the life of the Church, that of Synods and councils.

From the institutional point of view, it is not necessary to insist on the powerful role played by episcopal conferences in the transformation of authority in the Church. It will be protested, and in a sense it is true, that "Vatican II didn't want that," had not wished for this parliamentarianization. It is the eternal debate concerning moderate revolutions: Did Vatican II want that or not? In any case, without Vatican II, it would not have happened. The mold of episcopal conferences, instead of rehabilitating the personal authority of the successors of the Apostles, has on the contrary submerged their individual responsibility within multiform secretariats and diocesan councils of all kinds. In this arena, Gilles Routhier, in a thesis defended at the Catholic Institute of Paris and the Sorbonne,[14] criticized in the name of a failed ideal, the concrete democracy experienced in dioceses of Quebec in the mode of "an institutional adjustment to modern and urban society," the specialists of diocesan rectories constituting veritable decision-makers, on the model of their counterparts in business or administration, with well-known "defects and parallel hierarchies," manipulation of committees and "working sessions," channeling of discussions, etc.

The defenders of the most conciliatory interpretation of the Council would desire the institutionalization of this debate at the summit; their strength, however, is on the decline. But the constitution of the Church, as it has historically narrowed toward the pinnacle of the Pope, makes the combination of Roman centralization and old dogmatic habits the foremost obstacle to greater democratization. The Bishops' Synod, which assembles periodically in Rome, has remained up to now purely consultative, with its meetings supervised rather closely by the Curia. To this we must add the politics of episcopal nominations throughout the world as a force for maintaining a moderate majority. The centralizing Roman reflex has survived and even been strengthened to some extent by the charisma of Pope John Paul II, who enlarged his universal presence as much as possible.

In itself, however, centralism would not prove an obstacle in the march toward unity in diversity. It should be noted that those who desire a greater democratization of authority do not seek a profound institutional modification. Thus, Hermann J. Pottmeyer, in *Le rôle de la papauté au IIIe millénaire [The Role of the Papacy in the Third Millenium*, Cerf, Paris, 2001],[15] did not propose replacing the Fifth Republic with the Sixth, but only to "reanimate" a spirit: "to give another method of working to the Bishops' Synod" and to accord it the right of decision-making; "to recognize a greater responsibility in the bishops' conferences" (especially in the choice of bishops).

Basically, it would simply be a matter of establishing in the heart of Roman governance — the Curia, the Bishops' Synod — the practices of transaction and negotiation which have been established at the level of local churches. Having been fully installed at the summit, they would be even more fully imposed at the lower levels. It would be a question of making the center integrate fully the role of manager of diversity, notably of a certain diversity in the *Credo*.

These notions result from an ecclesial tendency that is a bit winded at the present time. But in principle, wouldn't the proponents of this tendency really like to be able peacefully to enunciate, publish, and teach everything, including the more qualified heterodoxies, without the least risk of exclusion? The only risk would be that of a warning or a prohibition against teaching or, more seriously, failure to accede easily to episcopal or curial responsibilities. In summary, there remains this fact: it has become impossible today to be excluded from the Church, a community founded on a confession of faith and a body of doctrine, for heresy.

CHAPTER IV

Continuing liberal pressure: the ordination of married men

"Madame, the Church is asking me to ordain your husband. Do you accept what this ordination is going to mean for your conjugal and family life?" This is the question which the bishop asks the wife of the permanent deacon at the moment of his consecration and which threatens one day to be asked of the wife of a married priest.

The demands of the most liberal wing of Catholicism, of the still well-entrenched and influential conciliar party, have never ceased. This is so even if new appointments have reduced its representation within the episcopacy and even more in the College of Cardinals. For example, Msgr. Kurt Koch, Bishop of Basle, took up the chorus during a television program,[16] saying that one of the solutions to the crisis in vocations is the ordination of married priests. It must be said that this tendency, which plays the role of "the party of innovation" in the heart of the conciliar world, has undergone a mutation analogous to that of the political left since the foundering of communism. It has abandoned entirely the "social" view and is henceforth devoted to an advance of "democracy in the Church" (not only institutional but psychological). The subtext of these claims is the adherence to and reclamation of the dominant ideologies.[17]

Well-entrenched pressure groups

This current is carried by Catholic opinion heavily contaminated by ultra-modernism. In the diocesan councils, in the heart of the bureaucratic workings of the bishops' conferences, in Catholic media, and in certain religious orders, it has benefited from the solid positions and support network enjoyed by the clergy who "implemented" the Council. Its hope has been not so much for the election of an ultra-conciliar Pope, but rather that of a man who would be more or less willing to go along with its demands.

Thus, everything has tended toward the belief that the discipline of the Latin Church regarding the ordination of celibates would be set on the agenda as soon as John Paul II's papacy ended, at least for France and certain neighboring countries. If so, it will mark a particularly significant indicator and even accelerator of the internal secularization of Western Catholicism and of the transformation of its institutional structure.

One occasionally hears French bishops affirm more or less openly that setting aside the question of ordaining women, the ordination of married men will have to be considered in the coming years, with caution, as an exception, as an urgent solution to the problems of shortage. If it were to advance, there would be two clergies, one celibate, the other married. This last would function in the world as a lay clergy, if you like, an aid ministry, a little like the current married deacons.

If the Apostolic Letter *Ordinatio Sacerdotalis*, rejecting the ordination of women, continues to feed theoretical discussions regarding its magisterial authority, it is nevertheless true that its practical content is not seriously challenged outside extremist circles. As I noted above, what really bothers the critics is that the Church takes a principled position that diverges from worldly ideas: it is the very fact of affirming the impossibility of such ordinations that is incomprehensible. But no serious person really envisions the ordination of women in France for a long time to come; it follows that it would provoke the breakdown of legitimacy in moderate quarters which the post-Vatican

II Church, in its ever more anemic state, could not tolerate. Quite different, however, is the claim concerning the ordination of married priests, which is pressed on purely disciplinary grounds. While these grounds are genuine, the consecrated celibacy of priests also has an immense religious and institutional scope and has always been considered part of the essential spiritual scaffold of the Church.

In this regard, celibacy's partial abolition would represent a heavy lien against the future of the Church. Certainly the change could in itself be considered as an accidental, of substantially less import than allowing the drift toward a pastorate that supplants the priesthood. But from other points of view, the mutation would be very serious, not so much because a degree of perfection would disappear, since the example of Eastern discipline could be invoked, but because the priest as such would disappear even more in a secularized society, advancing the self-obliteration that he had begun by abandoning his clerical habit. Because the abolition of celibacy would indeed be an ideological choice. This choice seems practically inevitable given the post-conciliar direction which no one seems willing to bring to a halt.

What is the future of the liberal wing of Catholicism, of what we could call the conciliar party? I will return to this point in Chapter VI, but the foundational choice of the past forty years, the "opening to the modern world," is subject to a double response at the extremes (one claim of principle, in the name of tradition; the other *de facto*, going beyond this and demanding the pursuit of change); and it is also subject to a double interpretation within the conciliar world in particular. On the one hand, there is a moderate interpretation, or if you wish a reformist one, of the Vatican II option, which was represented by the pontificate of John Paul II and in a particularly clear way in its late phase, by an important segment of the Roman Curia. On the other hand, a liberal interpretation, of the center-left type, still largely represented in the world episcopate and in the personnel who direct the dioceses, but also by another portion of the Curia.

At first sight, the correlation of forces appears to affirm a moderate interpretation of Vatican II. This is as much in the kind of renewal the secular and regular clergy is experiencing as it is in the activist character of the younger generations of Catholics who still attend church. In theory, time ought to be against the ideological edifice of "the spirit of the Council." Yet the last forty years weigh very heavily. Within the framework which remains in the post-conciliar wake, the reconstituted Catholicism of today, with its young troops of new communities, World Youth Day, volunteer outreach groups, seminarians, scouts, local parishes, and so on must be assessed accurately. The average young Catholic of today demonstrates enormous gaps in the most basic catechetical knowledge, goes to confession little or not at all, is very susceptible to the dominant behaviors of the boys and girls of his own age, and maintains a Sunday practice of worship that is very elastic and based upon his "needs" as an individual. As for the young priests and religious, if their good will is great, their vulnerability remains that of our contemporary Catholicism.

Whatever the case, as in every comparable ideological phenomenon, cultural power, which really inspires the movement of institutions over the long term, belongs to those who are the most in harmony with the fundamental ideology of the age. In this case these are the members of what I call for convenience the center-left or conciliar party. In effect, the simple fact of including them at the frontiers of the Church guarantees pluralism and even an eruption, notwithstanding the fact that the numeric and vital force is with the more moderate wing. The latter, on the contrary, paying only lip-service to the innovations, more or less against their inclinations, while seeking to corral them, are, because they refuse to extirpate the root, always ultimately frustrated in their hopes of "reviving the interior" (then-Cardinal Ratzinger).

It is true that given diminution of the ecclesiastic framework and the general tendency toward individualism, the artificial character of authoritarianism of Vatican II is running out of steam. At the heart of the anglicanization that began with the Council (the evolution toward an fragmented religion from the doctrinal point of view and the experience of a broad liturgical dispersion), the moderate tendency which I characterize for lack of a better term as center-right[18] is conceded a fair scope for action. But if the conciliar wing is obliged to jettison some of its ballast, it is because it holds with the general phenomenon referred to as "communitarianism" in current democratic society, and it desires the recognition of all the particular groups within the bosom of the social collectivity, as long as the great principles of this collectivity are not called into question. The center-right thus plays a moderating role, but one can also say it is useful to the conservation of the ideology it moderates.

It would thus be a serious mistake to underestimate the capacities of the utopian sensibility today, as much as it may appear to have withered. It is the more effective in that it has had to re-center itself.[19] The privatization of religion is one of the factors which leads to the defection of the faithful. It has not always been thus, persecution and a narrowing of the vital space often having spurred a spiritual vigor and apostolic increase. But today repudiation in the private sphere coincides with an accelerated dispersion. From the internal perspective, the shrunken terrain of official Catholicism remains more than ever heavily influenced by the "conciliar" tendency, especially at the level of the diocese and local councils and committees.

This is the more so since new habits play in its favor. A young priest, for example, newly arrived in a parish where he wishes to attempt corrections such as the suppression of altar-girls, or the reimposition of a more didactic form of catechism, or preaching directed toward the encouragement of individual confession, still runs up against a latent defiance, a kind of reflex in favor of the conciliar legitimacy on the part of the churchgoers, of whom a certain number are not at all "progressive."

In the name of "the right to the Eucharist"

I said in the Introduction that considering the number and average age of diocesan clergy, the number of active priests in many dioceses is going to fall in the coming decades to a truly minimal level. I also remarked that some people think this will automatically enhance the position of the new generations of priests, who will soon constitute the great majority. This is the dream of the "biological extinction" of their elders, the generation of '68 as they refer to them, that is nurtured by the young and future clerics.

The figures of annihilation of the priesthood obsess all those in the Church who retain their sense of responsibility. Is it necessary to add that the prospect of an increase in priests of a faithful frame of mind hardly appeals to many of them? Thus, the search for "other solutions" becomes the first order of business.

In fact, despite the downward spiral, vocations still exist in a number of relatively flourishing communities and seminaries. To put it simply: vocations flow towards communities that tacitly or expressly recuse themselves from the "spirit of the Council" or that try to evade the problem, which comes to the same thing. The fact that these entities, with all their weaknesses, exist, requires us to take them into account. And above all if, after the Council, vocations have plummeted eighty percent, the first thing to do regarding the future of the priesthood should logically be to pose questions about this event.

Meanwhile, the ever increasing urgency permits "the party of the Council" to put forward solutions that tend simply to blur the frontier between clergy and laity, so that the pastoral function (governance, distribution of Sacraments, teaching) falls largely to the charge of Catholics unseparated from others by consecrated celibacy. There are not enough priests now? The laity will come to the rescue! Is this not in providential conformity with lay participation in the life of the Church as envisioned by Vatican II? Driven by choices made forty years ago, a clerical solution paradoxically emerges: the dispersion of the priesthood into the flock of the baptized, concretely by the constitution of an intermediate corps between clergy and laity, that would become a type of second clergy. What's more, given the gravity of the situation, even moderate pastors are tempted to find temporary solutions here in order to avoid the worst.

In fact, the ordination of married deacons, whose generosity of commitment and services rendered are not in dispute, moves in the same direction. It is not generally known that the number of annual ordinations of permanent deacons in France (three-quarters of whom are married) is essentially equal to that of priests. These men, who because of the average age of the clergy will soon be as numerous as priests, are from the sacramental and canonical point of view clergymen, who preach, preside over a certain number of ceremonies, and are awarded various responsibilities. They have, nevertheless, family duties like the faithful laity and are like them engaged in an active professional life within a totally secularized social context.

Likewise there has come into existence an intermediate category of ecclesiastical personnel who appear under various appellations in the diocesan organizational charts: "acolytes" or "extraordinary ministers," who are charged with the partial administration of the Sacraments. To these ministers — men or women, among whom there are some religious, and couples in some cases — are delegated worship functions (baptisms, marriages, Communion, Sunday celebrations in the absence of a priest, burials, First Communions), by virtue of a "letter of mission" delivered by the bishop and a liturgical ceremony of investiture.[20]

47

It is also necessary to note the pastoral organizers (members of parish or district teams who work alongside the priests, responsible for chaplaincies, diocesan functions, catechumenate, etc.). There are also laymen who have received a "canonical commission" to teach in a seminary or a theological school, even to exercise official functions as judges, lawyers or auxiliaries of an ecclesiastical tribunal. Yet again: recently two women were named to posts of responsibility in the Roman Curia.

Furthermore, if most of the parishes and parish districts are equipped with a lay council that assists the priest on a consultative basis, canon 517 § 2 of the Code of Canon Law of 1983 also permits a "participation in the exercise of the pastoral care," in other words the very office of the parish priest, to be entrusted to the deacon or "another person who is not a priest" (a lay minister, a sister), or yet again a group of people. A priest, generally from a neighboring parish, is then named "moderator" of this pastoral responsibility, but it is not the priest of the parish. Today, then, the curial responsibilities (preparation of celebrations, catechism, burials, parish collections, membership rolls) are sometimes exercised, in France at least, by what is called the pastoral organization team.

The French diocesan Synods of the end of the 20th century have contributed considerably to promote this establishment of laymen in the heart of the clerical apparatus. They have had the effect of predisposing minds toward the passage from traditional clerical responsibility to a collegial assumption of that responsibility by a few priests and many laymen, this stemming from the fact that French Catholicism was in the process of becoming a Catholicism without clergy. The phenomenon is about the same in the United States. Generally, their most tangible result has been the creation of a permanent diocesan assembly made up of priests and laymen and the organization or reactivation of parish and inter-parish councils. Theology courses given by laymen, cycles of instruction by session or through correspondence, the fact that laymen study in theology departments and obtain canonical university degrees, all of this can powerfully encourage institutional mutations.

What next? Not a great rupture, basically not much: merely to enable the representatives of the lay clergy, of the second clergy which is in the process of consolidating itself, to preside over the Eucharist.[21] Bernard Sesboüé, S.J., professor of dogmatic theology at the Sèvres Center (Jesuit Faculties of Paris), a man of some weight who has the ear of certain dioceses of France, would propose a process whereby a bishop lays out for Rome the paralysis of his diocese and requests permission to ordain married laymen who are already theologically trained and who are at his disposal. (He didn't specify, but it goes without saying that he proposed this measure for what was then the next pontificate.) [22] The bishops, not necessarily the most progressive among them, refer to this "unavoidable" necessity, which Cardinal Martini had publicly evoked in 1994: it would be appropriate to renounce the Latin discipline of ecclesiastical celibacy "as an exception, in certain situations."[23] Aren't married deacons designated to form the first ranks of this new category of priests? If the discipline of the Latin Church were modified, fifty-four percent of them would immediately be ready to be ordained priests, if one is to believe a survey of francophone Belgian deacons.[24]

It is in this context that the "Instruction on Certain Questions Regarding the Collaboration of the Non-ordained Faithful in the Sacred Ministry of Priest"[25] made an appearance in order to throw up a roadblock. It was signed by no less than eight prefects or presidents of Vatican dicasteries; the document received an enthusiastic reception, even acclamations, in the majority of French seminaries. It dealt with one specific part of the priestly function. It recalled that it is "in virtue of a surrogate" that a layman can provide his assistance to priests who are not up to their tasks in this particular domain (symmetrically, one can imagine — and it is an historical occurrence — priests exercising political functions under the designation of "surrogate"). Voicing its major objective, the Instruction denounced the abuses which are found in the exercise of this substitution: homilies pronounced by laymen in the course of the Mass; confusion of vocabulary (laymen called "chaplains," etc.); laymen pronouncing words or using gestures reserved for the priest during the Eucharistic celebration; witnessing of wedding vows without there really being a lack of priests or deacons. It could be pointed out, besides, that beyond the specific abuses, such a reminder could correct a more fundamental drift: laymen have specific duties that are far more urgent than helping priests to say Mass or giving homilies or distributing the Sacraments!

But everyone knew that this call to order was a pure formality and that it could not be followed to any extent and thus was without effect. And above all, calls to order of this type are likely to carry little weight in the face of the "necessities" put forward by the adversaries of the Instruction: the faithful "have a right" to the Eucharist and priestly celibacy is merely an "historical variable"[26]; "renunciation of the imposition of obligatory celibacy" is indispensable[27]; "the continued refusal to envision the eventual ordination of married men will place the demand for priestly celibacy before the needs of the Christian community"[28] etc. In other words, the desacralization that followed the Council corresponds to an unforeseen fall in ordinations which therefore renders "inevitable" a new stage in the desacralization, analagous to monetary devaluation with its attendant downward spiral. Fr. Sesboüé, who considers that the Instruction had "a disastrous effect," concluded, "As for its future authority, that is an entirely different matter."[29]

Laicized priests, clericalized laymen

Hardly had the Instruction been published when Fr. Joseph Moingt, S.J., gave a provocative talk on "the future of ministries" in the heart of the diocese of Ars, whose seminary has been one of the most receptive centers for this kind of document.[30] He asserted that "a more democratic organization of our communities is highly desirable. This is not a theoretical or intellectual hope. It is simply that it appears necessary for the survival of our communities, for the witness that they must make." The old theologian continued, "For my part, I do not believe that we will resuscitate the recruitment of priests and religious without rebuilding this foundation of our communities. Responsible communities must be given all means possible to acquire a sacramental existence, since that is the very existence of our communities." There followed this consequence concerning the Eucharist: "Above all, every community must have the means of constituting itself in the Eucharistic celebration. A Christian community is a celebrating community." Fr. Moingt, however, did not thrust this point home, that is he did not completely abandon the notion of ordination. He imagined that the community could present a layman to the bishop, who would give him a "ritual sign," a "liturgical investiture," so that he could "conceive of those ordained to preside over the sacramental celebration of a community without having the personal or social character of the priest: they would not be inscribed in the *Ordo Sacerdotalis*, in the clerical order. They would remain laymen." Joseph Moingt thus straddled the question of the Eucharist.

On the other hand, he went the full distance with the democratic demand concerning penitential matters. Bulletin n.13 of *Documents Épiscopat*,[31] edited by Fr. Henri-Jérome Gagey, on the topic of "Ordained Ministers and Sacraments," quoted on page three and in note six a clearly more radical text by the same theologian, taken from *Courrier aux Responsables d'aumônerie*.[32] Fr. Moingt responded affirmatively to the question of whether the celebration of Confession presided over by laymen in the absence of priests could be defined as sacramental: *"It cannot be doubted* [my emphasis] that the pardon of God, celebrated in a

51

liturgical act but in the absence of a priest, is effectively received and is sacramental, and it is appropriate to signify it by the proper gesture accomplished by the pastoral team (in the ancient Church the 'kiss of peace' was practiced").

Fr. Gagey summarized the thought of Fr. Moingt saying that, in this case, "access to grace must be held to be *certain*" [my emphasis]. The heterodoxy of the proposition was precisely this *certitude*: "It cannot be doubted…" Indeed, to utilize language of traditional theology, it could perfectly well be said that a penitential ceremony without a priest can eventually be the means of provoking an "act of perfect contrition," and thus be a possible indirect channel of the grace of reconciliation. On the other hand, to affirm the *certainty* of the communication of this grace in such a ceremony is to make it the equivalent of the Sacrament of Confession conferred by a priest, one of its "efficacious" signs which, according to the expression of the Council of Florence "contain grace and confer it upon all who receive them worthily." (Decree to the Armenians).

Assuredly Fr. Moingt did not fall in a formal sense by an express definition or condemnation already made by the Magisterium; the Council of Trent takes aim, specifically, at those who say that even non-bishops and non-priests possess the power of the keys, or those who say that faith without repentence can result in the remission of sins *DzH* 1684-1685. His error regarding the Sacrament of Confession took a new form vis-à-vis the ancient errors. It was linked to a series of diversions: claims bearing on the possibility of Eucharistic celebrations without a priest, for example at the end of meetings in school chapels; on the possibility for non-sacerdotal hospital chaplains to confer the Sacrament of Anointing; on the possibility that these same individuals, who obviously hear many confidences on the part of the sick, perform the Rite of Reconciliation.[33]

In any event, it's not necessary to be a prophet to foresee

that the question of the ordination of married men, in the position of auxiliary priest, will sooner or later be examined publicly as a specific and supplementary solution. Except that the "second clergy" from which they would be drawn also suffers a crisis of vocations, and more generally the universal crisis of commitment. Paul Valadier, S.J., a realist, doesn't believe that the laity will be able to relieve disappearing priests as easily as claimed: the generation of Catholic Action is today itself moving toward extinction. "Without wishing to prophesy the worst," he adds, "it is necessary to predict that sharp internal conflicts will arise unless the current reciprocal indifference prevails, the two groups proceeding in ignorance of each other on parallel tracks."[34]

There is a big risk however that the new Pope, however moderate he may be, will be obliged to compromise with the liberal environment. It may be supposed that the practical decision to mandate married men to preside over the Eucharist and the Sacrament of Confession "as an exception" would then be left to local bishops, taking account of various circumstances and regional urgency.

Even at the margin, if accepted here and refused there, it would be a decisive step in the laicizing of the Church unfolding since the last Council and of the clericalizing of the laity going well beyond the worst moments of regimentation within the ranks of the pre-conciliar Catholic Action. It would represent an historical stage of the progressive effacement of the priest in modern times. It is often said, to explain and excuse the crosscurrents and "abuses" that followed Vatican II, that it would take time for a council to be truly enacted. It is true that several generations were required for decisions of an assembly like that of Trent to permeate the ecclesial body. The ascetic and spiritual reform of the clergy, of the dioceses, the reform of the moral and sacramental life of Christians, of the catechism, the rebirth of religious life, the restoration of the liturgy which followed this Council encountered substantial resistance. The Council ended in 1563; the reform of the clergy did not effectively begin in France until the beginning of the seventeenth century. Vatican II, an atypical Council, is not comparable to those which preceded it. However, while moving in the opposite direction from the Tridentine reform, the metamorphosis of the Church it has brought about has been similarly slow and laborious. The movement of "opening to the world" met and continues to meet with opposition, it is challenged by local or centralized attempts at "restoration," it runs up against harsh resistance. But to the extent that it has been able to take advantage of these difficulties to settle down and refocus, the ecclesial transformation ought logically to continue within the framework of a Church that is as diverse as it is enfeebled.

If one enjoys inverted historical parallels, he could say that the possible permission to appoint married men to preside over the Eucharist would be to Vatican II what the institution of priestly societies (Lazarists, Oratorians, Sulpicians, etc.) and the creation of seminaries were to the Council of Trent.

PART II

WHAT RESOLUTION?

CHAPTER V

The end of infallibility?

Is it too late to regain our course? If the confession of faith formulated by dogma still has any meaning, the Church today is virtually in a state of eruption. It is solely because the heterodoxy of Father X regarding the virginity of Mary, of Professor Y concerning the Resurrection of Christ, and of Bishop Z concerning the indissolubility of marriage do not draw consequences that they remain officially within the Catholic communion, along with theologians who profess a multiplicity of paths to salvation, who challenge the implications of natural morality in every domain, who express public doubts about the Resurrection, etc.

Attempt at coming to grips

It is no secret that the influential men of the current Curia, along with the high ecclesiastic officials worldwide who share their reflections, dream of firmly taking the reins. The present Curia, the most intricate seen since the Council, churns in a way that brings to mind the Curia before the Council, under John XXIII, multiplying documents that were polemically called "restrictive" (definitive prohibition of worker priests, condemnation of Teilhard de Chardin, obligatory Latin in ecclesiastical studies, preparatory texts of the Council that seemed to have issued from the pen of Pius XII). The Tardini-Ottaviani team at that time worked at cross-purposes with a history that was going to sweep away their efforts. What will become of those of the Curia Sodano-Ratzinger? It is a conclave being prepared and not a council, but a conclave which everybody believes, rightly or wrongly, will mark the beginning of a new era. The nucleus directing the Curia leans on the great documents of "restoration" of the pontificate of John Paul II: the new *Code of Canon Law*; Instruction on the Ecclesial Vocation of the Theologian; the new Catechism; the Instruction *Donum Vitae* and great moral encyclicals; *Profession of Faith* decreed by the Congregation for the Doctrine of the Faith; Apostolic Letter *Ordinatio Sacerdotalis* staving off the ordination of women; the encyclical *Ecclesia de Eucharistia* and finally the Instruction *Redemptionis Sacramentum*. *Ordinatio Sacerdotalis* represents a peak, because its form seems to approach most closely the dogmatic Magisterium of yesteryear, as if Vatican II had not occurred.

As if Vatican II had not occurred... But if their dream reached this point, it would be enough for the Roman officials to open their eyes to see that Vatican II is always very much there and more than ever blocks the horizon. It's not that the Council changed anything in the definition of ecclesial authority, but in some way it chloroformed it. A new pastoral mode, neither fish nor fowl, not truly Magisterium but quite a bit more constraining than the Magisterium, has been substituted for the traditional magisterial function, as we have seen, in order to allow for the strong but untraditional elements of doctrine, those which carry what is referred to as "the spirit of the Council," ecumenism, religious liberty.

Now in the Church everything rests on the Faith and its transmission, and the backbone of authority conferred by Christ to pastors is the teaching function. The root of the evil — and what evil! — a degeneration in which heresy springs up everywhere like mushrooms and where unity is lacerated everywhere — is not then in the weakness of the holders of authority. It is above all in the fact that they have forbidden themselves to grasp the rudder, that they have concretely renounced the act of binding and loosing along with the supreme authority, that of *judging* things of the Faith in the name of Christ. As if the ultimate Magisterium had been put on the back burner and in a cascading effect, all teaching authority, from that of the Successor of Peter to that of the last lady catechist, had lost all force of obligation. Consequently, each "picks and chooses;" the borders of the Church have become vague, and it is possible to profess heterodoxies while remaining within the camp. Whence also an indecisive and foggy teaching which permits the sign *par excellence* of full ecclesial communion, the Sacrament of the Eucharist, to be given to non-Catholics (*Code of Canon Law*, canon 844 § 3).

What distresses the high officials is not, at least explicitly, the uncertain direction of the conciliar path, but the response of the theologians who call everything into question, starting with moral teaching, supported by the bishops, followed or preceded by numerous laymen. In this situation of schism or rather of latent disintegration, it is easy to acquit the Council and dismiss the foregoing argument. The fruits are evident; the Church has become practically ungovernable. But the rulers and the opponents are forced by the democratic culture to live and struggle in the elaboration, the manipulation, the response and the interpretation of legislative texts.

From whence we have this succession of documents for "reining in," or to use a different metaphor, to try to plug the holes in the boat. Thus, after the new *Code of Canon Law*, the new catechism, the moral encyclicals, *Evangelium Vitae*, (March 25, 1995), *Ordinatio Sacerdotalis* (May 22, 1995), the Instruction on Diocesan Synods (July 9, 1997), full of reservations for their excessively bold innovations, the Instruction "on some questions concerning the collaboration of the lay faithful with the priestly ministry" (November 13, 1997), which tries to prevent the effacing of the borders between priesthood and laity, the Apostolic Letter *Ad Tuendam Fidem* (July 1, 1998), which inserts into the *Code of Canon Law* instructions concerning the authority of magisterial acts, the Apostolic Letter *Apostolos Suos* on the theological and juridical nature of bishops' conferences (published July 23, 1999), which delimits their doctrinal authority and gives value to that exercised by each bishop by virtue of his claim to be a successor of the Apostles, the Instruction "regarding the pastoral care of the divorced and remarried," the document on "the priest, teacher of the Word, minister of the Sacraments" of 1999, the encyclical *Ecclesia de Eucharistia* of April 19, 2003, which practically recalls the doctrine of the Council of Trent on the sacrifice of the Mass, the Instruction *Redemptionis Sacramentum* of March 25, 2004, which reproves abuses in the celebration of the Eucharist.

It can, nevertheless, be asked what was the use of having the cavalry officers issue endless edicts on the rules of riding if they never mounted a horse. With each promulgation, during the early period, the defenders of liberty urged a "permanent coup-d'État" against the violation of the spirit of the Council.[35] Later, they shrugged their shoulders: nothing fundamentally changed, this weak-kneed authoritarianism revealing itself as nothing more than "an admission of feeble power" (Henri Tincq); "spiritually and theologically unsustainable" (Paul Valadier), all amounted to nothing more than paper-shuffling.

One thing is certain. The documents and decrees never governed by themselves, whatever the opinion of the bureaucrats and their ecclesiastical counterparts. Who will govern in Rome, in the dioceses, in the communities, in the years to come? And how will they govern? The landscape may be renovated for better and/or for worse. The Church seems destined for an irresistible Anglican-style fragmentation. Yet at the same time the elements of rebirth — included undeniably in this very atomization — are more vibrant than ever in the past forty years: the proportion of Catholics who find their spiritual and doctrinal sustenance in places and communities of choice is ever greater.

God directs all things, yet without the free will of men ceasing to be necessary. This includes the free will of pastors. In a word, will they resolve to put the magisterial vessel back on course?

Procrastination

From this point of view, it must be repeated, the pontifical document that cuts most against things conciliar is *Ordinatio Sacerdotalis*. "In order that all doubt may be removed regarding a matter of great importance, a matter which pertains to the Church's divine constitution itself, in virtue of my ministry of confirming the brethren (cf. Lk 22:32) I declare that the Church has no authority whatsoever to confer priestly ordination on women and that this judgment is to be definitively held by all the Church's faithful." The sentence concerning the impossibility of ordaining women to the priesthood *resembles* an infallible definition. It could have been, yet it is not: the Congregation for the Doctrine of the Faith specified on October 28, 1995, that it is a matter "of an act of the ordinary pontifical Magisterium, *in itself non-infallible*, [which] attests to the infallible character of the teaching of a doctrine already in possession of the Church."

It seems that the pastors of the Church, pulled by the very momentum of Her functioning back to the edge of a chasm that was crossed forty years earlier, cannot make up their minds to recross it. But it is inescapable: to govern it is necessary to want to do so, in the Church and outside it; to *judge* sovereignly the matters of the Faith, it is necessary to have the will to do so (a little like needing to *want* to do what the Church does when accomplishing a sacramental act). This includes everything that comes with assuming a pastoral charge: responding to pending questions of faith (for example, can one give Communion outside of Church Communion?), settling the controversies on which they depend (defining, for example, the object of ecumenism), discerning and judging texts which are at the heart of the controversies (in the same example, to say what is grain and what is chaff in the conciliar decree *Unitatis Reintegratio*). Will they take the hard step?

The authorized commentary by the Congregation for the Doctrine of the Faith to the Letter *Ad Tuendam Fidem* intensified their paralysis. The Letter, published in July 1991, was in the extension of the Profession of Faith[36] and of the Apostolic Letter *Ordinatio Sacerdotalis*. These three documents had for their principal objective a precision intended to require the admission — perfectly traditional, despite dissenting theologians — that not only the truths which appear at first glance to be contained in Revelation but also the truths "which are necessary to keep and faithfully expound the Deposit of Truth" can be taught infallibly by the Church.

These truths are concretely the most important in the current debate. It emerges from the particularly elaborated commentary by the Congregation for the Doctrine of the Faith to the Letter *Ad Tuendam Fidem*[37] that these truths correspond to what theologians generally called "the secondary object of infallibility," or what they qualified as "subsidiary truths" to the revealed Deposit. But the commentary of Pope Benedict — then Cardinal Ratzinger — and of Msgr. Bertone, Secretary of the Congregation, deepened the theological reflection: certain truths, at the moment they were dogmatically defined by the Church, did not yet appear as formally revealed. It was the development of knowledge of doctrine which subsequently made it apparent that they were integral parts of Revelation. The totality of these truths tied to Revelation "add to the Faith," says the Congregation, "non-revealed elements or elements not yet expressly recognized": this refers to the classic developments in theological treatises, explaining that dogmatic formulations generally advance the intelligence of the Faith starting from a formerly defined element which is developed by a theological work; this ends in a new definition.

It is in such definitions of Popes and councils that infallible magisterial activity concretely manifests itself; activity which advances the formulation of the confession of faith contingent upon new questions that arise. Basically, heretics of every age have resulted from the non-acceptance of this "human" part that the living Magisterium seems to add to the Deposit of Faith in these formulations. However, the Congregation for the Doctrine of the Faith points out that even before being solemnly defined (and perhaps never to be defined), these verities linked to the revealed Deposit can perfectly well be taught by the ordinary and universal Magisterium (Popes and councils), which is infallible by the same authority as the solemn Magisterium (save for determining exactly its content).

These explanations have this as their object: to the degree that such a "subsidiary truth" (for example the condemnation of contraception or of the ordination of women) is already taught by the infallible Magisterium, it ought to be considered as definitive and indisputable. Anyone rejecting such a truth would place himself outside the communion of the Church. All of this is effectively unanswerable. But it remains to be determined whether or not it is contained in the infallible teaching of the ordinary and universal Magisterium as such: "No doctrine is considered as infallibly defined unless this is manifestly established."[38]

And it is here that the straits begin to narrow. The Congregation for the Doctrine of the Faith makes clear (in implicitly defining the laborious theological debates of the past) that only the solemn infallible teachings are characterized through a solemn definition.[39] By contrast, as infallible as they may be, the teachings of the ordinary and universal Magisterium are not presented by a definition. And thus, since they are not strictly speaking *defined*, it is substantially more difficult to determine if they belong to this category. Taking the case of the condemnation of contraception, if it is not part of the ordinary and universal Magisterium, it would be only part of the non-infallible authentic Magisterium; it would not be definitive and would eventually be reformable. Yesterday contraception, today the ordination of women, tomorrow necessarily other difficulties, without mentioning cases opened by the Council: it can be said that these truths linked to the revealed Deposit of Faith (or which seem to be subsidiary but perhaps are fully entitled to be considered a part of it), regarding which it is constantly necessary to make judgments, are the daily bread of the living Magisterium.

The drama of the post-conciliar Church is that everything concerning the reference criteria of the supreme Magisterium is frozen: no longer normative, but only "pastoral!" This destabilizes all the rest, because if the greater (the solemn Magisterium) is no longer practicable, how to know whether the lesser, essentially "undefinable" (the ordinary and universal Magisterium) is either? Let us suppose that it no longer is and that, in some way, the magisterial machine is "jammed." How then will the vigilance of the supreme Magisterium, normally ever ready to act and thus guaranteeing the smooth function of all teaching activity of the Church, be applied to the liturgical norms and texts, to the laws and canon rules, to the conciliar texts and others concerning the universal Church, in order to avert all risk of error? Conversely, if these texts sometimes cause spiny problems, isn't it precisely because the magisterial program no longer has the same characteristics and has allowed the introduction of a dangerous virus? If this is true, the situation is highly precarious.

But let us suppose that it is not like this, and that the magisterial mechanism functions after Vatican II exactly as it functioned before; it would still be the case that Rome and the dissenting theologians would remain locked in an identical arm-wrestling contest: how to force the admission that a truth linked with Revelation in virtue of a "historical relationship" or a "logical connection" is indeed infallibly taught by the Church, since no definition of reference is applied any longer?

Only by defining without definition, rendering infallible

without an infallible act. It is the dream of an infallibility that would erupt by spontaneous generation. But this mode of escape constitutes a coup against classic magisterial doctrine, to enter the field of theological novelties, the one explained by the Congregation being not merely novel but highly ingenious. It is the case, explains the Congregation for the Doctrine of the Faith, where the Pope, without making use of a solemn definition, can declare that a doctrine is part of the ordinary and universal Magisterium. And this textbook case is furthermore exemplified in *Ordinatio Sacerdotalis*.[40] By a non-defining act — and thus "*in itself non-infallible*" — the Pope "attests formally" that a doctrine is already a part of the infallible teaching as understood in the ordinary and universal Magisterium. And that is why the doctrine is definitive.

But how can the Pope, without being infallible, designate with certitude that it is infallible? The dissident theologians win the point that if the attestation is not infallible, no progress has been made in what concerns the attested doctrine, since the greater cannot issue from the lesser. It is possible to curve the angles; the circle remains stubbornly square. This is a search for a surreptitious infallibility that would establish itself automatically without an act of will and whose appearance it would be sufficient to certify; it represents the confession of post-conciliar impotence which it seeks to overcome. One could naively ask oneself: since they have taken the trouble to elaborate this authentic declaration with such preparation, bedecked in such solemnity and followed with such pointed explanations, why not simply have issued a dogmatic definition that would have put an end to the debate (provoking, undoubtedly, ruptures within the communion, but these will come sooner or later)?

We get the impression that those who are in charge of post-conciliar affairs (such as the theologians who prepared the innovative texts of the Council, and this undoubtedly explains it) have a fear of infallibility amounting to panic, as if its activation amounted to a nuclear option. God only knows what successive explosions, what devastating mushroom-clouds, what vaporization of the conciliar and post-conciliar universe could follow the fact of pressing the dogmatic "button"! It is as though the will to exercise the final and definitive Magisterium, to discern and to *judge* each time that it is necessary, has been anesthetized.

CHAPTER VI

"Last Pope" or transition Pope?

The real question then was not the one that was posed by journalists: *who*, after Pope John Paul II? But rather, *what* after John Paul II? The analysis and designations that follow will perhaps appear too political, indeed savor of political machination. But when we study the history of the Church, notably that of the councils, we are struck by the fact that the most important pastoral and doctrinal questions advance divinely in the midst of what humanly speaking are turbid political eddies, ambiguous or even base. The Church is both divine and human, directed by the Holy Spirit as much at the moment of the Great Schism as during the times of the holiest reforms, but always fully present in the most "human" situations.

Simply put, I think that we find ourselves, forty years after the Council, between two hypotheses, that of the "last Pope," and that of a transition Pope. Two main tendencies coexist, which for convenience and with awareness of the inadequacy of such terms, I designate as center-left (or conciliar party) and center-right. The two "extreme" wings are excluded from direct political involvement with post-conciliar issues, although neither is negligible in terms of influence: one of the right, unalterably opposed to the major orientations of Vatican II, traditionalism in the broad sense; the other of the hard left (in brief, the Greens and the Trotskyites of the Church), which is in the process of wilting. With the advent of the new pontificate, the action will be concentrated in the center, something recognized in both *Concilium* and *Communio*. Or more precisely, it seems to me that everything will be settled within the center-right, under pressure from and possibly in negotiation with the center-left.

The center-left

This conciliar party is the working wing of the ecclesiatic personnel who took power in 1962.

We may remember the surprising novel of Jacques Paternot and Gabriel Veraldi, *Le dernier pape (The Last Pope)*,[41] which recounted that following the death of John Paul II, his successor took the name of Matthew I. After having allowed priests to marry, buried the prohibition against contraception, authorized access to Communion by remarried divorcés, etc., he assembled a council to complete the work of Vatican II, in the course of which...he abolished the papacy and once against became a simple bishop. Some would term this scenario indecent, even for a fictional setting, noting that in the last analysis it is the Holy Spirit who directs not only conclaves and councils, but the entire life of the Church. Jacques Paternot and Gabriel Veraldi would reply that the Holy Spirit did not see fit to prevent the election of Alexander VI or of Julius II and that Providence permitted a whole period of papacy à la Machiavelli. There is no doubt that it allowed it only to prepare the way for a powerful awakening of the Church.

So why would it be absurd to propose a hypothetical election, if not of the "last Pope," then at least of a Pope who would cause or allow the old edifice to be transformed into a kind of democracy, with all the reactions and counter-reactions imaginable? Such a hypothesis was not absurd in 1998. One can imagine it happening today, but in a very muted way, which is by no means reassuring.

It is important to remember the thunderously sanctimonious declaration made by Cardinal Martini, then archbishop of Milan and head of the conciliar party, by way of a swan song at the

Synod of European Bishops in October 1999. It summarized the "pontifical program," which this tendency always endorses, no longer via its own candidate, which it is no longer able to elect, but by favoring the election of a compromise candidate. Without expressly pronouncing the word "council," Cardinal Martini proposed launching an "experiment of global encounter among the bishops," then enumerated in seven points the "kernels" which according to the conciliar party should be laid down (and which go substantially beyond "discipline"):

- ❑ resolve the problem of the "dramatic lack of ordained ministers" — in other words, ordain married men[42];

- ❑ review the "place of women in the Church" — in other words, give women access to the platform of the presbyterate, to the various "ministries" presiding over the celebration of marriages, of more or less sacramental penitential gatherings, and of the distribution of the Sacrament of Anointing and to the diaconate;[43]

- ❑ consider the problems pertaining to "sexuality" — to wit, hide *Humanae Vitae* under a bushel while appealing to the rights of the individual conscience;[44]

- ❑ scrutinize the problem of the "discipline of marriage" — in other words, permit "remarried" divorcés to receive the Eucharist;

- ❑ study the question of "penitential practice," that is to say favor as much as possible collective penitential practices and absolutions;

- ❑ revive "the relations with sister Churches among the Orthodox and more generally "reanimate the ecumenical hope" — in a word, give broad permission for inter-Communion and con-celebration;

- ❑ examine, finally, the relations "between democracy and values" — classic theme (see the Dagens report of 1994, cited above) of those who believe it possible to claim a privileged role for Christianity in the service of democracy.[45]

This last point is fundamental to the inner workings. The opening to the world that Vatican II desired will not be achieved until the Church has harmonized its functioning — with the specificity proper to its spiritual object — with that of modern democracy. This was the linchpin of the program enunciated during the same period by Fr. Paul Valadier in his book, *Un christianisme d'avenir. Pour une nouvelle alliance entre raison et foi*[46]: it is necessary "to introduce the elements of democracy into the life of the Church." And the commentators amplified the call as one would have expected of them (Cardinal Martini submitted his entire declaration to select press outlets, such as *La Croix*) in successive waves; daily,[47] monthly[48] they "translated" the message: Carlo Maria Martini asks for convocation of a permanent deliberative meeting, a council or Synod. It was clear that the particular themes of such a program were only incidental to the basic theme: that of advancing Vatican II in the sense of institutional evolution.

The classic echo effect now took hold. In December, Cardinal Eyt, now deceased, made a declaration under the pretext of responding to a talk that Cardinal Ratzinger had given in a Paris colloquium on the topic "Faith, reason, and the institutions of the Church." He declared in *La Croix*,[49] "The judgments demanded by the course of the life of institutions brook no delay or procrastination. Those in positions of responsibility are on the line." The Archbishop of Bordeaux cited the "kernels" urgently requiring definition as evoked by Cardinal Martini. Then it was Msgr. Karl Lehmann's turn. In an interview broadcast by *Deutschlandfunk*[50], the Archbishop of Mayence, president of the bishops' conference of Germany, explained that the convocation of a "third Vatican Council" seemed a given. On February 19, 2000, Msgr. Walter Kasper, Secretary (and future Cardinal-President) of the Pontifical Council for Promoting Christian Unity, gave an interview to *Die Welt*: "There are important questions in our Church to which the Pope probably cannot respond by himself."

Two demands effectively convey the transformation to be pursued: "collegiality" and "decentralization." Both, and the first in particular, have regularly been brandished at the three conclaves — June 1963, August 1978 and October 1978 — that have been held since the opening of the Council. The other conciliar wing, the center-right, which with Popes Paul VI, John Paul I, and John Paul II, wielded power in Rome, cannot confront these two themes directly: Paul VI as well as John Paul II and their collaborators worked ceaselessly for the collegial machinery of the Bishops' Synod to turn noisily but without effect. I will take up a discussion of the center-right shortly. It should be said that in themselves the two ideas can be completely legitimate: the extreme centralization of the Church and its maximal "papalization" encountered since the 19th century, which is explained historically by the climate of radical struggle between the Church and the society that emerged from the Enlightenment, are not of divine institution and contain plenty of drawbacks. We can perfectly well imagine — and even hope for — a Church where the Catholic bishops would recover a full and visible stature as successors to the Apostles in communion with the Pope, the latter exercising his Magisterium as universal bishop confirming his brothers in the Faith.

But in this context, these terms do not actually possess their traditional meaning: they mean, specifically, a modern type of democratization for the Church. Let it not be said, moreover, that the papacy envisioned by the center-left of the conciliar world has fewer powers than the current post-conciliar papacy. Centralism is not an obstacle to democratization, to the extent that it fully integrates the factors of a new legitimacy, in particular that of the "spirit of the Council." The post-conciliar notion of decentralization of the Church is not at all a throwback to ecclesial provincialism nor a raising of the responsibilities of each bishop, which could have disconcerting "reactionary"

71

effects, but rather the wholehearted adoption of consensual debate at the highest levels and governance by "aligned" pressure groups.

For the center-left ecclesial tendency, the ideal would be that the Pope who emerges if not from the next, decisive, conclave, then at least from its sequels in the medium term, act in the manner of a president of a State or a Secretary General of an international institution. He would eventually enjoy greater power than he has at present, but within a well-defined ideological framework and essentially democratic mechanisms (which can without much trouble be adapted to their responsibilities in the ecclesiastical rites of succession). If this were to happen, the Church would be molded in a brief half-century into the form of a presidential regime, without ever having known the system of constitutional monarchy by which the divine right regimes adapted to democracy. In this hypothetical evolution, the nominations of bishops could be made practically at the level of episcopal conferences and super-conferences, to which would be added representations of priests, ministers and involved Catholics.[51] From these Church assemblies there would emerge an appropriate Roman synodal representation with collegial power, which the Pope would have to take into account institutionally. For example, the Curia itself might function under the direction of a commission created by the world episcopate. The Pope, more conciliar than ever, would certainly be constrained by opinion networks but on the other hand would enjoy a much greater democratic legitimacy.

In this type of evolution envisioned by the conciliar party, far more important than the mechanical details is the harnessing of the power of opinion. From the launching of Vatican II by Pope John XXIII, it is ecumenism that serves principally as a lever and secondarily as the theme of the promotion of the laity. During Vatican II, the Secretariat for Promoting Christian Unity of Cardinal Bea provided the point of reference that the doctrinal commission of Cardinal Ottaviani ought to have provided. We know the importance of ecumenical and interreligious "gestures" for the functioning of the conciliar machinery. Dialogue is for the conciliar Church what the Rights of Man are for contemporary democracy.

"I am in complete agreement with Cardinal Martini," said Msgr. John Raphael Quinn, in an interview granted to the magazine *Jesus*.[52] The former Archbishop of San Francisco had published a book on *"The Reform of the Papacy"*[53]: "For me, it is fundamental that a future ecumenical council includes at least the Orthodox Churches as full participants." Likewise, Paul Valadier: "It is undoubtedly appropriate to envision the face of tomorrow's 'Christianity,' not in the guise of a hypothetical and improbable 'return' but rather in the form of a communion of communions, of a Church of Churches guarding their legitimate traditions and recognizing one another mutually in their very diversity."[54]

In all of this, isn't traditional doctrine being pushed around a bit more than at the time of Vatican II? Indeed, the most conciliar element of the propositions emanating from this tendency is the means used to redirect the requirements of doctrinal continuity of the divine constitution of the Church, namely the discovery of the "pastoral": a "pastoral" Magisterium, that is non-infallible doctrine. Theologians and hierarchs of the center-left hammer relentlessly that the decisions that bother them, such as those on the ordination of women and on moral choice, are "disciplinary." These will eventually be replaced by others, theoretically as little binding, but in truth revolutionary. Pastoral, pastoral: doctrinal orthodoxy can take it easy, conciliar forces are not acting *against* it, but *beside it*...

The simple agenda that the conciliar party will seek to impose is to continue the Council. Cardinal Roger Etchegaray thus issued a call to vigilance during the Great Jubilee: "Verifying the acceptance of the Council poises us for departure rather than for arrival.[55]" With dithyrambic verbiage, the former Archbishop of Marseilles exclaimed at Sinai on February 27,

> "Holy Father, from Mount Sinai to the hill of the Vatican, what roads traversed by humanity, by the Church in migration across a terraced desert of Abrahamic shafts from which Christ does not cease to bring forth the water of eternal life! We are here this morning, during this Jubilee year, at the edge of a vast and profound shaft excavated by Vatican II. And we cannot forget that you were here yesterday, as Father of the Council, one of the drillers of this shaft over which today you have the ecclesial charge of maintaining vigil with the diligence of a bedouin."[56]

The seasoned political observer Fr. Gianni Baget Bozzo analyzed for *Il Giornale*[57] all this orchestrated agitation prompted by the declarations of Martini: "All of that shows that the next conclave has already begun. The longevity of the Pope has forced the progressives to break their silence. And, in a certain way, the progressives have already established the order of business. It gives them a decisive lead [...] The battle of Vatican II was lost from the beginning by the traditionalists on the question of the agenda. This is the essential importance of Martini's maneuver: it fixes the conclave's agenda." It could be objected that Martini was "out of the gate too early." Indeed. Churchmen are very fine maneuverers, inheritors of immemorial experience. It was important for his constituency that he clearly set the milestones.

The Center-right

Opposite or to one side are the members of the center-right. This tendency, like the other, is a nebulous one. There are more than nuances separating, for example, Cardinal Giovanni Battista Re, Prefect of the Congregation of Bishops and a man of the establishment, and the restorationists like Cardinal Ratzinger, former "progressive" expert at Vatican II, became a traditionalist leader on the inside, a little like Chilean Cardinal Medina, former Prefect of the Congregation for Divine Worship, who has followed the same path.

Excluding the "extremes," who will carry the day, the moderates of the center-left or of the center-right? Regarding the papacy, it was highly probable that the smoke of the Sistine would announce an election from the center-right, since, from consistory to consistory, nominations of cardinals (like the bishops) have been made globally in that direction. The "progressive" cardinals' loss of influence was also palpable in the lack of repercussions following the interventions of Cardinals Lehmann, König, and Lorscheider in the consistories which followed that of 1999.

This having been said, things remain in flux. Within the center-right, everything will be determined, as I have suggested, between the two sub-tendencies that can be discerned and that I would qualify, with all necessary reservations, as restorationists and compromisers, these latter susceptible to pressure from the center-left. The possibility of the election of a compromiser Pope, that is, fairly conservative but open to the progressive demands, was very conceivable.[58] This was broadly speaking the direction of the pontificate of John Paul II. The direction adopted would then have been moderate but conciliar in principle, compounded of the *desiderata* of the liberal platforms. Would nothing be changed, then, relative to the case of 1978? Nothing, except that twenty-five years have passed since the election of Pope John Paul II and that the situation has deteriorated considerably. The status quo is assuredly the worst of the hypotheses. The vacuum of authority, much more evident, would render it even less possible to barricade against the demands that press so clearly in the direction of adapting to the dominant culture. These new adaptations would only increase the loss of internal credibility of an institution whose cohesion and means of governance are purely moral, except for the indirect support that the democratic "secular arm" can provide to the evolutions that it would be inclined to approve. This support includes police security at places of worship, ideological surveillance of communications, and various financial pressures.

Conversely, notably in France, the new clerical generation of young priests in Roman collar who have returned to the catechism, carried by the wave of World Youth Days and great assemblies, would reject having their hopes dashed. So that the other party of center-right, the restorationists, who occupy a fair number of command posts today in Rome, supported by Opus Dei, in sync with a certain number of new communities (Emmanuel, for example) and quite a few others of all the orders, could possibly prevail. They are fairly permeated with the themes of the traditional universe, especially in this: they invoke criticisms "from the right" to brake ecumenical overtures, showing that not only have these not achieved any pastoral advantage but they accentuate the rupture with the traditional world.

The struggle is so bitter that it resulted in a modification of the law of papal election. We must realize that a determined opposition to a restorationist candidate would seek to deprive him of the two-thirds plus one votes required. It was notably in an attempt to get around this obstacle that Sodano's faction pushed a reform to the law of the conclave by the Constitution *Universi Dominici Gregis* of February 22, 1996.[59] The newly rebuilt Saint Martha residence, not far from the sacristy of Saint Peter's, in providing very comfortable lodging for the cardinals, in effect permitted painless prolongation of the conclave, including through the heat of the Roman summer. The new law of election of the Pope authorized election by absolute majority at the end of ten or fifteen days of unsuccessful voting. It was not impossible that the restorationists would accede to this. Unless, as sometimes happens, the brilliant strategem boomeranged against its own inventors.

Given the election of a restorationist, we can pass from the hypothesis of the "last Pope," that is a more or less rapid exit from the traditional structure of the papacy, to the diametrically opposite hypothesis of a transition Pope, that is a progressive extrication from the post-conciliar papacy.

Is it not assuming too much, however, to suppose that the restorationists have the will to assume the burden of the failed pastoral and doctrinal experience of the past forty years? Certainly it would be absurd to claim that this will is expressly formulated. Furthermore it is asserted that the restorationists have no program, themselves. Is it possible for them to have one? John Paul II, at the same time the man of Assisi and of the new catechism, of the Repentances and of *Ordinatio Sacerdotalis*, of the disappearance of all constraining magisterial authority and of a presence never before attained by a Pope, has pushed to a maximum, aided by an extraordinary charisma, the union of contraries. But this "very polished" pontificate of John Paul II (again Baget Bozzo), which maintained a moderate interpretation of the Council against the background of the failings of Catholicism, is inimitable. "Our program is the Magisterium," the restorationists like to say, multiplying texts, as I indicated above, with which they want to believe that they will lock up the future and frame the course of conciliar matters.

To remain aligned with the "true Council," the "good interpretation" of Vatican II, such is the dike that they erect against their adversaries. It is true that they erect it also against themselves, as a limit not to cross in the other direction. In itself, then, even the durable installation of restorationist command would not imply any theoretical abatement of the Council. To put it yet more clearly, in the manner of Baget Bozzo: the election of a Ratzingerian Pope will not lead automatically to a process of *evacuation from the Council.* However, nobody can say what liberating effects the quasi-rupture of the very artificial current unity could bring. Logically, we would progress to a true and salutary separation.

Because a Ratzingerian Pope will necessarily be confronted with the problem of schism — for real — which it would be necessary sooner or later to declare. Otherwise, theologians, bishops, religious, authors and liberal media are going to continue to interpret the *Credo* and morality in their own manner, without ceasing to call themselves "Catholic," and the Church will pass little by little from the quasi-coma in which it finds itself to death pure and simple, or else the rupture will be consummated, as the survival of the Bride (and good sense) demands. At bottom, it is the proper virtue of the Pope to distinguish what is Catholic from what is not, and who is Catholic from who is not, and the Church must implore the Sovereign Pastor to grant this virtue to the Pope She has been given.

What is more, to speak constantly about the "true Council" and its "good interpretation," is this not inevitably to redirect the course of conciliar matters toward an *interpretation* in the full sense, a magisterial interpretation?

So that the declared adversaries of the Council (of its fundamental intuitions), the traditionalists of all stripes, despite all their weaknesses, play a prosecutorial role. The contribution of what they represent would be of no small importance to a revitalization of the remaining forces. Besides, a brew at all levels is beginning to form, that could very well become more defined under the pressure of events: at present, a common front uniting the Lefebvrists and other traditionalists, the "new priests," Opus Dei, members of the new communities, would still be difficult to promote.[60] But tomorrow?

CHAPTER VII

Tomorrow a common front?

No one is unaware of the rumors of discussions, then of rupture in the negotiations, then informal contacts between Rome and the Society of St. Pius X, pointing to an administrative arrangement. These sketchy, abandoned, and quasi-reactivated transactions are minor historical events, it will be said. Not in all respects, however. For the Church in France in its bloodless condition, the answer to pastoral needs of a community that accounts for around 300 priests is no more negligible than consolidating the future of the Community of Saint John [Translator's Note: the "Communauté Saint Jean" is a relatively new French conservative monastic community, unrelated to the now-defunct Society of St. John in the United States.] or giving pastoral responsibilities to an organized charismatic movement. Besides, whether they think in terms of "integration" or think about a pastoral contribution, the Church officials who are interested in the problem know that the community of Msgr. Lefebvre is merely the tip of the iceberg. They also think about the totality of the traditional world and beyond that the sum of all Catholic sectors — of which they themselves are a part — together with the liturgical and doctrinal demands which run counter to what Vatican II has represented in these sectors.

An outstretched hand

These secret negotiations, or efforts at negotiations, are suggestive of a fresh start and can point to new arrangements. For five or ten years, they seem to have been in the making. An initial stage of the post-conciliar period, corresponding more or less to the reign of Pope Paul VI, brought an eruption, followed by a second stage designated as "restoration," corresponding to the beginning of the reign of Pope John Paul II. The current period, beginning in 1985 and especially since the mid-nineties, represents a kind of movement to the limit, an unstable equilibrium ready to break. It is necessary to repeat that the ecclesiastical reality, at least in the West, is that of an unprecedented failure. This condition goes back a ways, but only recently has it been acknowledged; this has definitively put a halt to the ideological optimism of the "marvelous springtime of the Church." For those whom I designate the members of the conciliar party, there remains the forced march ahead, as they rejoice over the fact that the disappearance of priests is an "opportunity," that the anti-Christian secularization is a "challenge," etc.

But for the others, in particular for the most uneasy among those whom I designate restorationists, yesterday fervent followers of the announced renewal, today severely disabled, it is time for a sad settling of accounts. I have spoken about the catechetical crisis and the new plunge in the number of vocations. The phenomenon is not uniquely French. In the United States, a decline of the same magnitude occurred between 1965 and today (90 percent fewer seminarians), a decline that is more important in reality if one considers that the number of Catholics has grown during the same period by twenty million people. This wounded Catholicism has in these last years suffered a shock that can scarcely be measured in Europe, a shock provoked by moral scandal, and by the spectacular resignation of a conservative bishop, Cardinal Law, all of it obviously inflated by the media. In Switzerland, which like Austria, Germany and Holland saw the practical schism of groups resulting from an ultra-liberal Catholicism (didn't we see a Sunday gathering in francophone Switzerland applaud their priest who announced during his sermon that he was moving in with his partner?), there are practically no more entrants into seminaries in recent years. In Spain, the lack of entrants affects some thirty dioceses. Italy, preserved to this point, is being affected in the same way: the situation is that of a tardy but equally radical meltdown (for example, one of the most prominent seminaries, that of Milan, maintained its enrollment until around five years ago; then a steep decline occurred, followed, in typical fashion, by a veritable collapse within the past two or three years).

The time of disillusionment had begun well before it was acknowledged publicly, but people remained locked in a half-hearted attempt at "reining in" which didn't satisfy anyone. Now, as regrettable as it is to see the Church divided into factions, it is a fact that the group of those whom I refer to as restorationists, who are those more or less disappointed with the Council, is in the process of making gains in numbers and relative tenacity. They represent an entire array of people, of whom many, without daring to recognize it, have transmuted their disappointment by slapping traditional vision and practices on top of the conciliar novelties. The Roman Curia is more than ever highly diversified, not to say fragmented; it is possible without exaggeration to talk about a breath of panic that has seized many of its actors regarding this situation. One portion of them maintains an ever more open hostility regarding the liturgical reform as it was elaborated. In Italy, this question had apparently remained secondary, yet the media that criticize the reform, like *30 Giorni*, seem to find an ever greater echo in the clergy.[61] Also in Italy, a phenomenon is spreading which had previously confined itself to France: young diocesan priests are seeking to learn to say the Tridentine Mass.

As I said, a true common front, bringing together the "traditionalists" of all shades with young priests of a faithful frame of mind and with members of new communities, is up to now structurally improbable, but it is clear that the boundaries are becoming ever more permeable in a clergy that is wasting away as a body. "New bishops" and "new priests" are ready to utilize the greatest freedom of maneuver in a situation of "ideological weakness," in particular the quasi-official collapse of the dreams of the conciliar aftermath.

Consequently, in Rome, the criticism that has emanated from traditionalist milieu, even if often deficient in the way it is presented and far from unified, has never been better received. Those disappointed with the changes announced forty years ago are ready today to concede many things to the adversaries of the Council, not only in order to have allies "on the right" as they try to gain further influence, but also in order to prepare the future of the Church. In a word, today those disappointed in the Council are insistently extending a hand to those opposed to the Council.

In this context an event has occurred that, without being major, is nevertheless very significant: the creation of a customized apostolic administration, with a bishop and then a coadjutor, for the priests and the faithful of the Priestly Union of St. Jean-Marie Vianney in the diocese of Campos, Brazil. It is the decree *Animarum Bonum*, of January 18, 2002, that gave this group the status of a particular church assimilated to a diocese.

Without going into juridical detail, the apostolic administration of the Priestly Union of St. Jean-Marie Vianney has some relationship with the "military ordinariates" that organize the military members of a country and their families and, more remotely, with the Personal Prelature of Opus Dei. Such an administrative agreement could, it is true, be construed equally as a decisive advance in the criticism of the Vatican II reform or on the contrary as a victory of this reform which integrated partisans of the old liturgy into its bosom. This creation of a "personal prelature" is all the same a legitimization, or the beginning of a legitimization, of the rite of St. Pius V by the authorities of the rite of Pope Paul VI. "The spirit of the Council" today is very

82

much enfeebled, even though it continues to disturb ecclesial life, and to that extent the "recognition" of the St. Jean-Marie Vianney enclave of Campos represents events that destabilize the conciliar ideological totality. Because other "Campos," in Europe and in the United States, yet more favorable to the adversaries of the Council, could well follow on its heels.

Indeed, if we consider the administrative arrangements that have been negotiated and concluded since 1985, there has been a progression — logically, given the deterioration of the general situation — in the concessions afforded by the Roman authorities and a corresponding diminution in the "proofs" asked of the traditionalist communities (or, what comes to the same thing, in the concessions to which the communities believe themselves obligated). It can also be noted that each agreement has produced a double effect: a classic rallying reaction, that is an adherence to the Council by those who were "recognized," going beyond, at least verbally, what was asked of them; but inversely a reinforcement of their gains.

A necessary evolution of one and the other

In the course of discussing the gains made by the opponents of the Council, this theological observation can be made: all the Sacraments are ordered by the Eucharist (baptism in order to receive it, ordination to confect it, etc.). So the Mass is the final object of the celebration of the other Sacraments. Holy Orders, then, are linked to the Eucharist in numerous ways. The crisis in vocations which has assailed our country is first of all an extremely serious loss of the real sense of the Eucharist. Under a completely different aspect, the demand for a form of celebration like that referred to as St. Pius V — and what it represents doctrinally — implies a priestly and episcopal commitment in the same direction: priests are necessary to celebrate such a Mass and bishops to ordain the priests. It must be added that if the concrete modalities of the designation of a bishop have varied greatly in the course of the ages, the intervention is always *collegial* in one way or another, if only in the fact that (normally) the new bishop is sacramentally consecrated by three of his peers.

Mass, priests, bishops: links in a chain. The celebration of the pre-conciliar Mass now forms a part of the religious landscape, especially in France. The law in place concerning this form of celebration remains the following: in the heart of the new liturgical law instituted in the continuation of the Second Vatican Council, a simple but relatively broad tolerance was accorded by the *motu proprio* of July 1, 1988, *Ecclesia Dei Adflicta*, in favor of the Mass known as the Mass of St. Pius X. The publication of the *motu proprio* was placed in the context created by the episcopal consecrations of Msgr. Lefebvre of June 30, 1988. Because of these events, it made two dispositions: it instituted a commission charged with settling the status of priests and religious who had links with the Society of St. Pius X, individually or in communities, by conferring the possibility of celebrating the liturgy according to the missal of 1962; and for the faithful attached to the liturgical forms previous to the Council, it asked for the application of the terms contained in the circular letter of the Congregation for Divine Worship of October 3, 1984. According to this letter, the bishops had the faculty of using an *indult* (in canonical language: a grace carrying a dispensation from the common law) to allow the use of the 1962 missal.

In their totality, the stipulations of 1988 transfer the agreed-upon arrangements to the terms of the protocol of agreement signed on May 5, 1988, between the the present Pope, then-Cardinal Ratzinger, and Msgr. Lefebvre — afterward denounced by the latter — namely, the faculty of using the liturgical books predating the conciliar reform and the institution of a Roman commission to settle the various problems of integration of the members of the Society of St. Pius X. Concretely, the most notable element of the application of the *motu proprio* under the aegis of the commission established for this purpose has been to create or confirm communities that recruit priestly vocations for the celebration of the traditional liturgy.

It was still necessary for the bishops to want to ordain such priests in order to assure the continuance of the traditional celebration. In truth, there has never been a lack of active or retired bishops to respond to the "market" for priests included in the "market" for the traditional Mass. The celebration of this Mass, which everyone knows goes against "the spirit of the Council," survives — it is in the order of sacramental matters — by the commitment of bishops, whether "non-official," like those of the Society of St. Pius X, or "official." But these latter have proceeded and do proceed to ordinations for the pre-conciliar rite only a step at a time, and not as "Tridentine bishops." The crucial point of these 1988 negotiations was precisely the question of St. Pius X bishops: it was the announcement of episcopal consecrations by Msgr. Lefebvre that was decisive for the conclusion of the protocol signed between himself and then-Cardinal Ratzinger, and it was the autonomous execution of these consecrations that provoked the publication of the *motu proprio*. The pressure of the episcopal question has continued in some form in the concurrent existence of the Society of St. Pius X furnished with bishops and the diverse communities connected with the *Ecclesia Dei* which lack them.

But in 2002, the gap was closed with the nomination of an official "St. Pius V bishop," with the creation of a custom-made apostolic administration. In fact, the decree of 2002, *Animarum Bonum*, as previously the *motu proprio* of 1988, *Ecclesia Dei Adflicta*, afforded concessions for the non-conciliar Mass which had first been offered to the Society of St. Pius X. A decisive foothold involving the divine constitution of the Church, that of the episcopate, was gained. These particular concessions had been proposed December 29, 2000, by Cardinal Dario Castrillón, Prefect of the Congregation for the Clergy and President of the Commission *Ecclesia Dei*, to Msgr. Bernard

Fellay, Superior of this Society, and the offers remain viable. The expected pastoral and political interest overrode the active resistance. This latter expressed itself strongly in the French episcopate, supremely interested as it was in the officializing of the entire traditional world, churches, places of worship, schools, and religious communities, and also in Rome, among the ranks of the most fervent defenders of the liturgy of Paul VI and what it represents.

The opposition of the French episcopate was not unanimous, however; far from it. Besides, the physiognomy of this episcopal body has continued to evolve due to recent nominations. The condition of human frailty (and sometimes financial: from 2002 to 2003 certain dioceses have seen their charitable receipts decline by half), if it doesn't push diocesan bishops to seek out personnel in traditional communities, it does invite or oblige them to leave them greater living space.

The continuing non-acceptance of Vatican II in its most concrete form — its liturgical non-reception — ought paradoxically to have made inroads as a result of episcopal collegiality. But because the prospect of an official recognition of the Society of St. Pius X has grown remote, at least in the short term, that of a St. Pius V bishop issuing from the traditionalist world has also receded. Yet it follows the coherence of liturgical matters — and Church matters — that the celebration of the Tridentine Mass has called into existence Tridentine priests and that of Tridentine priests that of Tridentine bishops. In this sense, one can imagine one or several St. Pius V "ordinariates," similar to military "ordinariates" or to personal apostolic administrations for faithful of the oriental rites outside their country of origin, to which Tridentine communities existing or future might be linked. Except that the Tridentine liturgy is not one rite among others, but an antecedent rite that subsists beneath a subsequent rite and thus, concretely, one rite concurrent with another. Its celebration is, *nolens volens*, a transplant rejection of the *lex orandi* of the last Council, of liturgical reform, and definitively of the conciliar innovations themselves. Great questions of faith thus ripen in the heart of historically mediocre episodes.

No less logically, and regardless of the extreme segmentation of those who, in varying degrees, do not accept Vatican II, there is movement toward a global treatment of this doctrinal and/or liturgical non-acceptance of the Council. The most "conciliar" frankly concede that they understand that henceforth it will be necessary to "put up with" the traditionalists. As for those disappointed in the reform, they are getting used to the idea of an alliance with the opponents (in fact or by right) of the Council. This possible meeting of the *disappointed* and the *antis* invites an evolution of the one and the other.

On the part of the officials of the Roman Curia and of a certain number of bishops, this ought to be a doctrinal evolution. This could appear major, but in a good number of cases will be only the passage from the implicit to the explicit. Since they criticize the new liturgy almost openly by means of the theme of "reform of the reform," they must move to a more fundamental theme, which necessarily sustains the first, that of the *confirmation* of the Council. It is only too clear that it has produced impasses in all perceptible domains, and not only in the liturgy. If then it is agreed that the *lex orandi* of Vatican II should be reformed, it follows that questions must be asked about the corresponding *lex credendi*. The transient psychological stage could be — and I will return to this in the conclusion of the book — to admit those who question the legitimacy of Vatican II to "Catholic equality" as such. In a word, it is a matter of a classic and very delicate transformation by one side and the other, where those who have long been regarded as the guardians of *freedom* confer legitimacy upon those reputed to be *enemies of freedom*.

On the part of the traditionalist groups, it is a "pastoral" evolution that will logically be demanded. Paradoxically, it is likely that this will be harder to put in place than the foregoing. It will be necessary for them to leave behind the current mindset, mental although certainly real, of a perpetual relation of opposition between them and the conciliar world, in order to enter the framework of an alliance in which they would come to the aid of the disappointed conciliarists. From this perspective, to speak only of the liturgical question, these traditionalists will have to second the reintroduction at a more or less high dosage of the mysterial and sacrificial element (altar toward the apse, prayers of the Roman offertory, etc.) in the celebration of common parish Masses. This is not to say that these traditionalist groups must bury their received talent: the Tridentine rite will need to play the role of witness and benchmark for the liturgical tradition.

Given that in the short term the dearth of priests is increasing, it is necessary in the nature of things to imagine formulas other than the current parish grid-pattern. It is also necessary to keep in mind that, as I noted at the beginning, a good part of French Catholicism is organized in networks in order to survive. The installation of associations of priests, of communities of religious, or diverse organizations, the better to take charge of the vast territory inhabited by Catholics, is highly desirable. In the best scenario, the priests of the St. Pius V rite of various orders, having ceased to be treated as pariahs, dispense intelligently constituted pastoral care in the form of catechism, preaching, and works. It will be necessary to accept their contributions, among others, as instruments of reconstruction.

CHAPTER VIII

The pending liability

The reflections of this chapter relate to a future that is very difficult to capture except in a relatively general way. They assume that in the years or decades to come, the ecclesiastic disruption that followed the last Council will be on the mend. This supposes a scenario of *transition*, an eventuality whose "political" possibilities I have described in the preceding chapters and of which I will speak again in conclusion.

In any event, the expiration day is approaching. We can infer it among other things from the obvious failure of the innovations, the liquidation of what could be designated the conciliar party, of the very strong pressure of the secularized world against a Church ever weaker. But we can also infer it from the very feeble pastoral success of the use of mass communication on which the pontificate of John Paul II largely rested, a pontificate which was a kind of final weapon in the arsenal of the project of Vatican II. More deeply yet: the Church today finds herself in a state of latent and multiform schism, encompassing a multitude of confessions of faith issued and taught simultaneously, which is an ever less tenable situation. If this were not to end soon, it would become necessary to admit defeat because the Church would have definitively lost her mark of unity.

Given this scenario, how and at the price of what ruptures will the magisterial parenthesis opened by Vatican II be closed? Naturally, it is impossible to say, any more than we can describe the state in which, after the predictable shocks, the religion of Christ in the Western world will be found.

A democratic way of being

It is, however, already necessary to assess one of the major difficulties to be overcome at the time of reconstruction, which is of the order of the "structures of sin," these being mainly mental structures. The legacy of the present crisis situation will weigh very heavily for a long time to come, including during the reestablishment of the foundations of internal order undermined by the same crisis. It has become only too evident that the Church is ungovernable at an institutional level. But the root of the evil is found at the level of the Catholic soul itself. Essentially, it must be repeated that the specific link that unites the body of the faithful — adherence to a teaching issuing from Christ, through his intermediaries the Apostles — has been undone, not because of a classic crisis of disobedience, but because a democratic mode of being has become metaphysically integrated. This then goes beyond the fact that in the social life of the Church each exercise of authority and each implementation of discipline has become problematic, as we has seen in other times. It also goes beyond the independent exercise of judgment with which the *Credo* is recomposed by everyone. It is the very *capacity* of adherence that has today become diluted, *Rousseau-ified*. This dissolution of discipline, as much practical as theoretical, even more than the disappearance of the priesthood, would undermine the Church as a visible institution. It is necessary, then, to say at the outset that it involves a radical problem of faith, of ability to believe, that is to say of conversion, which must never be lost sight of in examining the social and psychological aspects of the malady to be cured. Because all the institutional or sociological agendas can only capture the surface of things in the Church. She remains inseparably human and divine, and Her supernatural *visibility* is transmitted through carnal channels.

My considerations, which could be modified by many unknown factors, concern only French Catholicism, of which it can certainly be said that it represents an approximate observatory for the entire ecclesial reality, notwithstanding the homogenizing effects of internationalization. This state of Catholicism is the reality in which we live, pregnant with the Catholicism of tomorrow. Furthermore, my observations can appear very pessimistic. To tell the truth, the "pessimism" which today often has replaced the obligatory "optimism" of the preceding decades in certain clerical discussions, isn't worth any more than the latter and is definitely in retirement. If we like, let us be profoundly "optimistic" to the degree that we consider the state of a Church which in principle has passed beyond what currently afflicts Her. And above all, from the concrete point of view of responsibility, we must confront the question: what to do? What to do, for example, to rehabilitate in a practical way the sense of dogma, or else the respect for hierarchy, that is to say, sacred authority?

Finally, I could be reproached here (and not only here) for wanting to lecture the bishops and pastors of the Church, who are and will be charged with these questions. But it cannot be otherwise; clearly, any discourse of this kind, mine or that of others, is addressed principally to them. "For by divine institution and the rule of the apostolic office each one together with all the other bishops is responsible for the Church," says the decree of Vatican II which concerns them.[62] Every discussion about Church reform is addressed to the successors of the Apostles, who have each and every one the care of the universal Church, in participation with the Bishop of Rome.

To assess the importance of the liability to be assumed, it is necessary to consider the depth of its cause and to repeat that the core of the critical situation of the post-Vatican II Church relates to a muting, on the part of Her own pastors, of what She is: it would have been unimaginable for a conciliar text to be titled in 1965 like the encyclical of Pope John XXIII, only four years earlier, *Mater et Magistra*. Everything has happened as if those who are in charge of the teaching of the Church had been seized with doubt whether the Church of Christ is the unique and total mistress of Truth. As we know, the doubt is related to the qualifier ("unique and total") but first of all, more radically, to the essence ("mistress") of Her who teaches with the very authority of Christ. In the general framework of the "opening to the world," a neutralization of the traditional doctrinal function has in effect been operating. The conciliar gathering adopted an attitude of voluntary abstention from its function of supreme teaching — the famous replacement of the dogmatic by the "pastoral" — which can be described as a kind of magisterial retirement, with the intention of easing the way for this "opening."

The situation thus engendered from the ecclesiological point of view will bring heavy consequences regarding the Faith: by a true, although careful, renunciation, those who were charged with declaring the Faith as an obligation have preferred to express themselves on lesser grounds. That has permitted them to "nuance" traditional doctrine, avoiding (or so believing) the reproach of rupture or dissonance, since they have placed themselves on a level other than that of defined doctrine. With the intention of attenuating the lines of traditional doctrine as much as possible, the bishops of Vatican II cultivated an ambiguity that permitted them to compromise with the reigning liberalism, allowing themselves to be carried by the general current. But the concrete effect was to cast aside the evangelical power of "binding and loosing," in other words, dogmatic power, judged "tyrannical" by modern consciences, and to install a kind of a-dogmatic life-form, which it is plausible to believe will last for a long time. The *negatio*, in this domain, has the value of *privatio*, since the new generations are more ignorant than hostile, or else are hostile by mere conformity. It is also necessary to take into account the transformation of the external ideology, which has moved from the strong discussions of the modernist mindset to a weak postmodern form, with a dissolution of all norms or counter-norms.

In this regard, the relativizing of Thomism, an element of the crisis which should not be minimized, is explained undoubtedly by a certain fossilization of the earlier teaching, but it is essentially connected to this fundamental relativization of dogma. Even if it is true that theological systematizing adds nothing to the Gospel, it lifts human knowledge, rational by nature, in an integral manner. Traditional scholastic theology was vulnerable to the charge of a certain sclerosis, especially in the way in which it was taught in the seminaries, but the object of criticism leveled against it was really the "rigidity" of the way in which the message was formulated, essential to the scholastic method itself. It was the very way of *thinking* the Faith that was shaken in its foundations.

From the related point of view of discipline, we have witnessed the resurgence, as I said, of what Pope Leo XIII had condemned in his Letter *Testem Benevolentiae* (1899), namely the introduction of a certain liberty in the Church, the restriction of the power of the hierarchic authority, with the result that each of the faithful can very freely develop his own initiatives, all on the model of "modern liberty," an essentially negative liberty, founded on contemporary society. One of the major legacies of Vatican II is the prevalence of this conception. It involves the situation of the Church in the heart of a pluralist democracy that is regarded as absolute.

Ideologization and emancipation

Furthermore, beyond the impregnation denounced by Leo XIII, the approval conferred on the founding principles of Western society[63] could not fail to produce consequences, which will probably endure within ecclesiastical society. Vatican II was followed by a collapse of discipline that subverts the sign of unity that is characteristic of the Church of Christ. This invasion by the spirit of the world, manifested by a relaxation of

93

morals and relations of obedience, is and will most assuredly continue to prove costly to souls: if the most serious challenges to dogma and their moral consequences are today issued freely, it is because institutional disorder permits it, but it is first of all — aggravated cause and effect of the disorder — because there is generalized indifference regarding the weight of truth. More broadly, it can be said that imprisonment within modes of thought that are alien to the constitution of the Church (in the functioning of its collegial, diocesan, and parochial structures) has produced a double effect of ideologization and carefree emancipation.

The ideologization itself has two aspects. On the one hand, it is a matter of replacing the authority of faith by a perfectly intentional authoritarianism on the part of, notably, the officials at Rome. Since, in effect, the supreme Magisterium has ceased to intervene as such, the teaching of the Church is no longer elevated beyond a qualified instance of authentic Magisterium, a non-infallible Magisterium but one which the Roman authorities have presented as indisputable. Now, in questions of faith and morals, that which is not irreformable and infallible is by definition (eventually) reformable, and thus (respectfully) disputable. A legitimate and fruitful freedom of theological research demands that reception with definitive submission not be compelled of those hierarchical teachings which do not call for it. The tendency to give a "practically" infallible and thus indisputable authority to the authentic Magisterium, especially the moral Magisterium, thus has rested on very weak positions. Which gave ammunition to dissident theologians crying "tyranny," in very bad faith it goes without saying, in the heart of their almost total impunity. This has weakened the authority of all authentic reminders of the Deposit of Faith, including within non-protest milieux.

On the other hand, and more consistent in reality, a tyranny exercised by the conciliar ideology has been installed: the pastoral sub-dogma has become an ideological super-dogma, the very event of Vatican II allowing only for "celebration" and the new orientations of this Council permitting only acceptance without discussion. They have so to speak reset the counter to zero, which has forced the readjustment of the remaining doctrine of the Church. This ideological tyranny, particularly significant since it has been taken over by the most conciliar people and milieux, cannot help but leave persistent traces.

One can speak of neo-Catholics. It must be said again that my observation point remains that of France, and that it does not claim to embrace the entire reality, even if numerous elements are transposable elsewhere. It should not be believed, moreover, that in speaking of neo-Catholics, I am establishing an implicit rupture between a category of neo-Catholics, carrying a negative value, and Catholics in the old style, who would implicitly enjoy a positive reference. I speak of Catholics today who — not all, but to an important degree and in any case very visibly — are profoundly Protestantized by virtue of disobedience, including those within the traditionalist world.

The imprisonment of the Church in a democratic framework has, in effect, provoked a consequence apparently opposed to the tyranny of which I have just spoken, but which is really subsidiary to it, that of a liberation from all ecclesial direction, legitimate or not. Every document of authority has been considered not as rigorously directive, but as providing a platform for debates. This is the most evident point: the self-paralysis of the Magisterium, which characterized the last Council, has been transformed above all into the quasi-impotence of all authorities, particularly but not only in the framework of their traditional exercise. In reality, the power exercised since the Council is different regarding its mode, and often regarding the instruments of traditional power. This is logical: the Church, within the framework of the "spirit of the Council," could not help but integrate increasingly the functional mode of

95

Western societies, namely a governmental mechanism by means of opinion, which is manipulated by pressure groups of all kinds, notably in the framework of multiple assemblies and councils and also by means of public discussion — open and controlled — via the media.

That has led to a curbing, both active and passive — which is to say, accepted by the authorities themselves — of all hierarchical life properly speaking, including that which directly concerns the teachings of faith and morals, sapped permanently by press campaigns or noisy publications of protest literature. The concrete ecclesial functioning has been transformed by this life of meetings which has been the Church's since Vatican II, in parishes, in dioceses, in national or even continental entities and in Rome. The "democracy in the Church" has been installed by the pastoral teams, the various department councils, and better yet the diocesan Synods (a fashion which is, nevertheless, in the process of eclipse).[64] As for bishops' conferences, everything has been said about the parliamentary mill that they constitute and which has contributed much to submerge the personal responsibility of the successors of the Apostles. At least until now — it is possible that things are in the process of changing — the episcopal personalities at the national level have broadly speaking been managed and enclosed within the framework of commissions and assemblies of the bishops' conference, and in their diocesan milieu, by the diverse councils of officials and representatives named, elected or co-opted.

Nevertheless, forty years after Vatican II, the climate of debacle and of lassitude, and also the relatively greater weight of a sensibility defined by a faithful adherence to the historical Church, have led to the fact that the intellectual dictatorship of a certain militant progressivism shows signs of exhaustion. But that fact as such and for the present does not result in a reversal of direction. The new structures and habits have established a kind of legitimacy which is also new, the more durable in that it is moderate, whose weight appears incapable of being lifted. It is rather an arrangement of positive modifications (a more dignified liturgy), at the same time as an exhaustion of the democratic reform (for example, the ever decreasing success of diocesan Synods). And above all, it seems that the spirit at every margin accords with the model of ultra-individualism.

Here is to be found the veritable trump card of the most "conciliar" tendency, otherwise numerically weakened, hierarchically much less represented, but whose principles of free discussion are, it seems to me, shared by everyone today. And this will consequently be the great obstacle to clear away in order to undertake a reconstruction. The rootedness of what are properly speaking modernist conceptions is profound, and the conquered positions will be difficult to overcome given the fact of democratization.

Catholics are thus inhabited by a state of mind which manifests itself most strongly as an unawareness of what the Magisterium is. This ignorance is involved in a circular and mutually reinforcing relationship: those who ought to formulate this Magisterium are dubious about its relevance in the modern world; the "subjects," inversely, have developed the habit of no longer granting obedience to faith because it is never demanded of them. What will happen tomorrow when the members of the hierarchy start once more to demand specific adherence to teaching as issued in the name of Christ?

Conditional adherence

Well beyond the issue of obedience, there is a much more general lack of acceptance which presently affects religious life, in the relations between priests and bishops. Disobedience and revolts certainly have always existed, but the climate today is that of a conditional obedience accorded a superior, that is to say an obedience emptied of its content. In effect, the liberal model of "common law" — the Church being one association among others — has been integrated psychologically by Catholics, so authority is considered by them, and by itself, as being exercised within an associational framework, that of the religious institution, of the college of priests, and the Church Herself, in which one is as free to abstain as one was free to integrate oneself.

This is the consequence of a movement from hierarchical order in the Church (Pope, bishops, priests) to a structure made up of multiple and concurrent networks. From this fact, the individual is obliged to "construct" for himself, as the sociologists say, the modalities of his religious adherence. Neo-Catholics, apart from their conservative or progressive sensibilities, henceforth have great trouble assimilating in their mental categories that a commitment can be definitive, whether it refers to marriage, priestly life or religious life. The most solemn oaths are regarded by them as always subject to revision. Inquisitorial democratic society, in addition, exercises supercilious vigilance in this regard, and it is easy for one who wishes to challenge ecclesiastical constraint, especially that of a religious institution or community, to make a direct or indirect appeal to this inquisition under the indictment of "sect."

It is also necessary to consider the recoil phenomenon rooted in the fact that authority is exerted very little: people are unaccustomed to obey. That produces a loss of benchmarks, a *Ratlosigkeit* as the Germans say, a dismay among the faithful who no longer know which saint to venerate, in the midst of a climate of generalized suspicion.

The weightiest problem regarding future reconstructions is thus that the sowing of the Word of God is in danger of falling on ground that is full of the brambles of a tardy modernity, that of the reign of inconsistency and irrationality. It will be necessary to proceed to a re-education (in fact an education), for example to a traditional liturgical practice and catechetical doctrine. It will be necessary, in truth, to explain and justify a lot of things that seemed previously to run on their own.

In so doing, one will run up against a profound deficit of general and religious culture in the new generations. And morally, this re-education will also stumble over the fact that a good number of those who admit Church doctrine accept it for themselves as a personal choice, that is removing its intrinsically and universally binding character. It is the personal decision (certainly indispensable under any assumption) to receive the Gospel and to live according to its message that becomes, definitively, what the scholastics called "the formal object" of the faith, instead of the authority of God revealing itself.

Effort will thus have to be exerted, one could say, *ad extra* and *ad intra*. On the exterior, because it is desirable to free oneself from the mesh of democratic participation. How to rehabilitate the sense of obedience, if not in rejecting first of all the democratic lie that in reality is no more than the occult governing of oligarchies, and thus in beginning by seriously revising the knowledge that we have of natural political realities? Is this conceivable in the Church in the short term? That will depend greatly on the manner in which the hierarchic order is reestablished at the beginning and what will remain after the great convulsions that we may anticipate. Will the "little flock" to which the Church undoubtedly will be reduced be liberated by confrontation with the powers of authority? We witness in countries like Poland the decay of the dream of rallying late Christian democracy, and this will undoubtedly provide a strong boost to this remnant.

On the inside, it is hopeful to note the beginning of the auto-destruction of this Church of functionaries engendered by the generation of Vatican II, which had a notion of obedience that was much more functional than religious. Nevertheless, an authority that wants to reestablish itself as such, at whatever level, will have to face subversive practices aimed at destroying or sabotaging its action, given the emplacement of protest mechanisms, notably through the proliferation of pressure groups. The more so as internal democratic ferment will be assisted by external pressure, which the "secular arm" will continually exert via the media. Given all this, we must not allow ourselves to become frozen in a mentality of reaction. In this regard, the theme of "true and false tradition within the Church" could be developed: tradition is not the repetition of formulas and recipes from before Vatican II. Neither is it an artificial "return to the sources" which would claim to span a whole segment of the past in order to return to hypothetical pure forms, as was sought paradoxically in the liturgical reform of Paul VI. One could say that it is a fresh reflection on the Deposit transmitted from generation to generation, so that it is effectively and vitally transmitted to the present generation.

One thing in any case is certain: this effort of reconstruction will have to make plenty of room for reflections about the future of the priesthood. The great question will remain that of the preaching and teaching of the Faith (catechism, liturgical life, preaching about life lived in conformity with the Gospel). The problem of the ecclesiastical renovation is that of the clarity of the word of the Church as such. The faithful and above all the non-faithful or infidels, a flock needing pastors, must be instructed.

All the Catholic sectors, including those that are apparently the most clerical, are "laicized," touched as they are by the apparently inexorable character of the disappearance of the priesthood, and more profoundly by the annihilation of all hierarchical sense. Yet there is no Church without priests. It is certain, though, that the "new priests" — the only ones who will remain in a few years and among whom "new bishops" are already being chosen — will not be sufficient for the task. They will need to have the qualities necessary to construct the framework of the laymen who will help them in various tasks, notably catechetics and evangelization, that they will have to fulfill (in geographic conditions that will necessarily require some rethinking, as I have already remarked; undoubtedly, habitual regroupings in some centers and episodic priestly presence in peripheral communities). These priests, those of France in any case, are products of their era.

The concrete state of the second generation after the Council also presents characteristics that must be taken into account. Since it is an absolutely decisive matter, it is necessary to go into some detail. The qualities of piety and good will of these new pastors, their desire for rupture with the preceding drift, have a downside, which produces a certain fragility (corroborated by the number of departures from the priesthood that occur after several years). First of all, they are very few in number and feel it deeply. Even if they enter the seminary older than their elders were, after having completed university studies or their equivalent, or even after having worked at a trade, they suffer in a certain number of cases from a certain immaturity, characteristic of their generation, at least in their capacity to take on situations that require substantial perseverance. Their vulnerability is explained partially by the fact that they come from sheltered milieux (urban families of four or more children, relatively well-off, enjoying protected social or religious options), certainly no cause for blame, but in which they are not prepared for a very unnerving "hard landing."

The demoralizing pastoral life of today often delivers a very rude shock: even if they anticipate the voracious maws that await them and try to protect themselves against being reduced to the role of administrators, they are nonetheless consumed by exhausting activities, they carry the weight of popular indifference — even if it is not universal — and they encounter very great solitude. Because they have had to pick and choose in their own formation, they tend to behave the same way in priestly life. One might think that the mistrust with which they are met by the priests of the preceding generations and the mistrust they themselves feel toward their elders will pass, but it remains true that these "new priests" have not really had superiors nor a guiding and protective ecclesiatic environment. They are a generation without fathers.

It must be added that the dramatic decline in recruitments eventually produces an effect of which we are beginning to become aware: the lowering of the intellectual life of the clergy. The time to read, except for a few magazines, and the possibility of studying have become non-existent for most of them. Furthermore, whatever their level — generally university studies — the general crisis in education cannot help but be felt by them, with its deficits in the matter of the formation of the intelligence, a situation which predisposes them to a moderate relativism or a fundamentalism which is hardly any better, and sometimes both simultaneously, depending on the subject.

All in all, it is clear that superiors and trainers — that is, reformers — will be necessary for these clerics, and this will require talented and attentive leaders and pastors. Think, for example, that with the best will in the world, in the matter of marriage morality, most of them profess the moderate laxness which has been diffused by teachers considered to be the most respectful of Roman teaching (namely, the theory of gradualism in the matter of living in sin: to absolve penitents while recommending a "tension toward the norm"). Thus we are presented with a double difficulty regarding knowledge of moral theology and the virtue of fortitude, which will raise a certain number of moral questions in preaching (and the sacramental concomitants, notably the pastoral and the confessional); these are crucial because of their confrontation with the world of practical atheism.

It remains to be said that there cannot be a reform of the Church that is not based on a human reorganization. We can look to a Tridentine reform without desiring an exact replica in a radically different context. The problem of *adaptation* or *inculturation* of Christian preaching today is totally different from what it could be in the most varied historical or geographic circumstances, because it concerns men who are molded by a new culture and new "structures" that are intrinsically foreign to such preaching. Reform was necessary during the sixties of the last century and still remains to be implemented, but in conditions that have become more difficult because of a worldly invasion wholly different from that to which the Gregorian or the Tridentine reforms applied their remedies.

A transition toward an exit from Vatican II

It is reasonable to believe that the days of exclusive power for the "spirit of Vatican II" are numbered, if only because of the evident exhaustion of that famous spirit. From now on we must think increasingly in terms of *transition* between the present post-conciliar state and the reorganization of the Church in a substantially traditional mode, but one which probably will not look much like what it was in the 1960s.

The adversaries of the major initiatives of Vatican II have often thought that it is considerably more important to reestablish the traditional Mass than to debate the Council. This is neither totally true nor absolutely false. The present crisis is first and foremost doctrinal, and it is quite regrettable that the attackers of Vatican II are too often preaching only to the choir, as they devote all their energies to the liturgical battle.

It is certainly true that the new liturgy enjoys a legitimacy that was born of Vatican II. The Mass of Pope Paul VI contains the "spirit of the Council," a little in the way the Council of Trent said that a Sacrament contains grace. Attacking the new liturgy — everybody knows or feels this — is to attack the Council.

When Pope Benedict, then-Cardinal Ratzinger, and his allies criticized the "excesses" of the "Mass of Bugnini," no one is unaware that they were obliquely attacking the foundations of the new order. When a young priest reverses the altar that had been facing the people, the negative reaction on the part of activist laymen in his parish is motivated by the fact that the measure is "anti-conciliar." When a bishop gives permission to a group of faithful to celebrate Mass according to the rite of St. Pius V, he realizes that despite all possible precautions and restrictions, he has created a non-conciliar enclave in his diocese.

And speaking of permission, is it necessary for traditional and conciliar Catholics to continue negotiating? Is this not to surrender to the drift of democratization and the interplay of pressure groups? If it is necessary to negotiate, let it be at a higher level, that is, clear debate in order to prepare the transitions for the future. For all those various traditionalists opposed to the "spirit of the Council," the moment is approaching to request much more than "permission" — and something quite different from "recognition" — from the Roman authorities who are worried about pastoral debility, or from bishops who truly wish to be pastors of their flock, or of superiors of communities. They must deal for example with the liturgy of the Church as it is celebrated in parishes. As for the communities, fraternities, and priestly unions who request "authorizations" and "indults," it is becoming imperative that they prepare themselves for something other than pastoral activity for relatively isolated enclaves. The hour has rightly come for dialogue at the heart of the Church. But for that to occur, they cannot continue to be oblivious of one another. Catholics of good will must talk to each other, to Rome, in dioceses and at all levels. No one today has the right to allow any opportunity to slip by.

Finding a solution is urgent. Using several elaborations, I have proposed the scenario of a *transition* to be organized between the present situation of the Church, hinging on Vatican II, and a subsequent state that would be sought as a pathway out of and beyond the conciliar age. This essentially concerns two domains, that of the liturgy and that of doctrine. But we could also talk of organizing a transition vis-à-vis discipline, the day-to-day life of the Church, and the formation of priests.

I would thus like to close by specifying, essentially in the field of doctrine, how I for my part conceive this "exit" from Vatican II.

It is relatively easy to imagine *transition* in the liturgical domain. It is not with regard to the preserved places, which must continue to be preserved and multiplied, but with regard to the ordinary parishes that something must be done. Certainly, many hurdles will be overcome with the recognition that every priest has the right to say the Mass that predated the liturgical revolution, and "St. Pius V-style" parishes or their equivalents will be established. But it is necessary above all that every pastor have the possibility of reintroducing a traditional spirit into the ordinary liturgy: sacrificial Offertory, celebration toward the apse.

No one believes in the possibility of a universal restoration, everywhere and all at once, of the traditional liturgical forms in ordinary parishes, forms which moreover might be somewhat different from the pre-conciliar. It is therefore clear that it is necessary to imagine progressive transitions and organizations. What is required is gradually healing the spirit which presided over the fashioning of the new liturgy, ultimately retrieving a certain number of its interesting experiments (for example, the expanded cycles of reading from the Old and New Testament). This project of evolution of the reformed rite toward a non-reformed rite moreover gains adherents under the rubric of "reform of the reform." The officials of the Church would implement it by rectifying the rite of Pope Paul VI in accordance with the Roman liturgical tradition, that is to say concretely in the direction of the rite of St. Pius V, which would remain a point of reference.[65]

A doctrinal *transition* is more difficult to imagine. Certainly, a liturgical "reform of the reform" implies a "reform of the reform" from the doctrinal point of view, in the sense that the deficiency of the liturgical reform is the mirror of theological problems and that the doctrinal haziness is visibly expressed in liturgical vagueness. If then one is moved to a gradual correction of the liturgy, to reverse the direction of the altar, to reintroduce the prayers of the Offertory or their equivalent, one will also be led in the same direction regarding what is similar from the doctrinal point of view.

As a result, a complete reconsideration must be undertaken of the theoretical principles that have destabilized the edifice for forty years. This could be focused particularly on an examination of the principles of ecumenism, which prevent a real and therefore truly fruitful dialogue with separated Christians. Earlier I recalled the weaknesses of the decree *Unitatis Redintegratio*, from which the practical result was an "imperfect" ecclesiality conferred on the separated churches: specifically, because of the salvific elements in these churches (baptism, orders), the decree *Unitatis Redintegratio* concludes that these as such — as separated — have a "significance in the mystery of salvation," and that the Holy Spirit uses them as "means of salvation." In reality, what there is in the separated churches that is beautiful and good, and which is eventually salutary for those baptized individuals of good faith who are to be found within them, belongs to Christ and his Spouse without spot or stain, the Catholic Church. Christ cannot have multiple spouses, a "first" spouse and "imperfect" spouses. Even though it is necessary, certainly, and much more so than in the past, to explain ourselves to Protestants, Anglicans, Orthodox, members of sects, with a great respect for persons, it is clear that the first respect owed to all is to dialogue on a sound and solid basis. It is impossible to escape a critique of the ecclesiological fuzziness that surrounds the ecumenical initiative.

It is true that it is difficult to imagine a progressive transformation of the expression of truth. In fact, the principle of a doctrinal *transition* such as we have discussed is analogous to that which makes liturgical transition admissible and thus desirable. In particular, it is necessary that the intention of the pursuit, the re-traditionalization of the rite, specify the stages which, considered individually, could seem marked by excessive secularity. These stages will be perfectly acceptable for all, given the end in view, that is to say the return to a rite that has become *lex orandi*, the profession of faith in worship. A liturgy in the course of "traditionalization" is already a traditional liturgy.

In the doctrinal domain, the ultimate objective of a "reform of the reform" is the elaboration of an authentic interpretation — by precisions, corrections, condemnations of wrong directions — of inconsistent, hazy or defective points. The objective is the return to the exercise of the Magisterium strictly speaking, the expression of the teaching Church as such. Before this authentic interpretation arrives, we may pass through various intermediary stages, and we must recognize that these teachings to be interpreted do not involve the teaching of the Church, but first of all the legitimization of a free discussion of the points in dispute. And at the same time, or before, the acceptance of non-adherence, for reasons of conscience, to these conciliar teachings. Here, I repeat, there will be the crossing of a decisive threshold: when those who cannot embrace the badly constituted innovations will no longer be denied the label of Catholic. Such people would include, for example, those who do not recognize the principles of ecumenism as orthodox.

This recognition by the responsible officials — or at least by that group I have referred to as those "disappointed" by the Council — could appear unacceptable because the formerly repudiated traditionalist elements would be admitted to the Church with parity. Paradoxically, legitimizing the criticism of ecumenism would ratify the fact that the Church is, indeed, in a state of ecumenism. This would be the case if it were done in community where the incompatible propositions ("good interpretations" of Vatican II vs. non-adherence to a certain number of propositions of Vatican II) would in themselves have the right of existence and expression. But precisely the essence of the entire process of *transition* is to be a deliberate passage toward another state, in particular toward a new ecclesial situation. Both the "disappointed" and the "antis," who among the varying tendencies represent something less than vast battalions, will have to consider one another in good faith and extend one another good will, since they will both be expressly engaged in this march toward an authentic interpretation of the disputed doctrines. All, in the scenario of a process of *transition*, await the definitive instruction of the Church. What is there to fear?

Truthfully, there is no reform except within a reawakening of faith and a movement of spiritual conversion. If then we often conjure up the small numbers of men and the perspective of a new Church of the catacombs, it is also necessary to remember that the most important thing is good will, that of the poor in spirit, who have hunger and thirst for the things of God.

History has shown that situations of extreme crisis, such as the persecutions of the French Revolution, can reveal to the faithful and their pastors who lived in an apparent state of mediocrity a capacity to rise to events with supreme selflessness, including martyrdom. This possibility is never to be discounted, and the lists of martyrs of the century that just ended will perhaps be longer than any of the others. In reality, the Christians of tomorrow will be confronted even more than those of today with a persecution that is particularly enveloping from the psychological and moral point of view. This is a persecution originating in a saturated consumer society and the exacerbation of individualism which point ever more insistently to a tyrannical reductionist conformity. We already see this tyranny taking the form of hateful legal and judicial pressures. But the heroism required of the reformers of tomorrow is not different from that of their predecessors. It is simply that of sanctity.

Benedict XVI and the transition

Forty years after the end of the Second Vatican Council, the succession of Benedict XVI to the Throne of Peter inaugurates, *nolens volens*, a phase of *transition* for the Church, that is to say a process of exiting from the atypical state in which this Council had placed Her. It had certainly been possible for this event not to have taken place, at least at this precise moment. In an earlier chapter, I examined two hypotheses about the future that it was possible to formulate a year before the passing of Pope John Paul II and that in fact represented the two faces of his pontificate. The first scenario envisioned the election of a "last Pope," that is to say of a cardinal who was moderate but open to liberal demands, who would have "continued the Council" by making a kind of democracy from the old edifice, or allowing it to be made, in the name of the demands of "collegiality" and "decentralization." The second scenario, diametrically opposed to the first, could and indeed did produce a "transition Pope," suited to undertaking a gradual disengagement from the conciliar universe. In both hypotheses I foresaw eventual collisions and ruptures, probably healthy ones in the scenario that actually transpired, like the pruning of dead limbs.

It is important to be clear: my analysis of what the election of Pope Benedict XVI would bring in the normal course of events makes no claim of being prophetic. No one can say in what way or how rapidly this "exit" will be accomplished in the course of this pontificate. We can, for example, speculate that it will trace a jagged course, with decisions and events that are still very conciliar, punctuated with decisive returns to the great tradition of the Church. At worst, we could even imagine that at the end of a certain number of unexpected turns of events, the hopes raised by the beginning of this pontificate would be aborted. In this case — albeit improbable, considering everything that the person of Joseph Ratzinger brings with him — it would only be a temporary setback. But this "exit" must come about sooner or later, not only because of the divine promises made to the Church, but most immediately because of the ever greater pressure exerted by an unprecedented pastoral failure: Catholicism has gone through many crises, but it has never been so profoundly wounded in this way. If we were not talking about the Church of Christ and if we were to judge the situation by Her visibility in many places, we could indeed believe that She is is mortally wounded. This quasi-effacement or disfigurement of the Christian religion in the oldest countries of western Christendom — voluntary in part, the famous "spirit of the Council" consisting precisely of this — represents not only the context of the election of Benedict XVI but also its cause: his peers clung to him as to a buoy in a shipwreck

To take only the example of the priesthood: extinction in Western Europe, terrible bruises in the United States, moral dissolution in other parts of the world. The satisfaction and the solace that followed this election in many sectors of the Church are dangerously enervating: the state of Catholicism, steeped in secularization, is such that the most determined election of "restorationists" resembles a last resort rather than a true vital leap. Nevertheless, conditions can now be established — notably in the form of a lucid assessment, wherein things will be called by their proper names — that can finally bring about this vital leap.

It must not be imagined that Benedict XVI will concretely call into question Vatican II. Everything tends toward the view that he will seek to "out-distance" the forty post-conciliar years rather than to reverse them. But he is the last person not to recognize that in seeking to save the Council in a Catholic manner, he will make it lose its radical particularity among ecumenical councils. Given the nature of the Church, the weight of events, and an ever-greater expectation, we can only turn immediately toward full interpretation of the driving elements of the "spirit of the Council": separating the wheat from the chaff. We must also note that the markers of this interpretation have been placed in all the documents of the previous "restorationist" teaching, not only under John Paul II, but following the Council itself, and are even in the very conciliar texts which sanctioned the "opening to the world." It has been said and repeated that the conciliar teaching — that which is conciliar properly speaking, that is, ecumenical in the broad sense — was by nature ambiguous: this ambiguity could also play and in fact now does play against it.

It would be too much to say that the election of Pope Benedict XVI was inevitable or to claim that the reversal it implies will necessarily reach its fulfillment. I only state that an event of this kind could only be produced within a relatively brief period, in the same way that the evolution it announces, even if it is strongly opposed and beset by all sorts of obstacles, will unfold more or less rapidly. Without adopting a Tolstoyan view of the "fatality" of historic events, one can all the same agree — above all in what concerns the Church, which possesses the words of eternal life — that an infinity of factors coming together establish in a given historical moment a kind of current that imposes its direction. Thus the confluence of what *Humanae Vitae* in 1968, *Donum Vitae* in 1987, the universal Catechism in 1992, and the Apostolic Letter *Ordinatio Sacerdotalis* in 1994, among others, represented, would have manifested itself sooner or later or in a different way. But the long road of return to dogma — which is still far from complete

— against the opposite movement, imposed by the "pastoral" Council, of placing the magisterial function in a parenthesis, simply had to happen.

Equally, taking into account the personality of Joseph Ratzinger, twenty-five years at the helm of doctrine as dean of the Sacred College of Cardinals, the immense emotion aroused by the illness and death of John Paul II, Cardinal Ratzinger's successive talks constructing the dramatic scenario of the state of Catholicism and the priesthood, the cardinals' votes affixing themselves irresistibly to his name during the extraordinarily extended preconclave period, followed by a dazzling election, it was possible for all this not to have happened at that moment, or not to have occurred like that. Everything came together, nevertheless, in a general direction which, sooner or later, would lead to something definite.

Since April 19, 2005, everyone has been scrutinizing every act and gesture of the Pope in order to prognosticate regarding the paths he will decide to take. But it seems to me much more significant to note an element, among many others, that does not depend directly upon his election. The context, at once catastrophic regarding the situation and positive regarding the reaction, shows that the advent of Pope Benedict XVI is part of the general movement of things currently. The year 2004-2005 was undoubtedly the worst there has been for French diocesan seminaries, entrants never having been so few, three among them (out of a mere fifteen) choosing to close their doors in June. And simultaneously, one by one, those establishments that retained a "conciliar" direction have passed into the hands of a consciously Catholic professorial body: in October, it will be the turn of a seminary in the southwest.

Toward a Benedict XVI generation

Many ask themselves if the new Pontiff will find within himself the capacity to govern an institution that has become ungovernable. The answer would clearly be no if it were a matter of governing by force. Since I am emphasizing the present current of Church history, we will already have remarked that Benedict XVI has a very particular political genius compounded by a "charisma" that is much more considerable than many thought, which permits him precisely to catalyze and guide Catholic expectations and reflexes more solidly and much less emotionally than John Paul II. He has seen a wave of popularity in his favor since 1985 (*The Ratzinger Report: An Exclusive Interview on the State of the Church*) that is very different from — indeed, complementary to — that from which John Paul II benefited. Today he enjoys a completely solid base among broad sectors of the faithful, of the clergy, of movements, many ecclesial organizations, and in a notable portion of the episcopate.

Logically, this base should increase and become more defined. Nominations (and hopes for nominations) for bishop, cardinal, and to the various diocesan offices, are really the final domain through which the power of the conciliar Church is exercised at all levels: how many candidates for bishop and then for a high position within the episcopate have fitted their image to their aspirations. Changes in the Holy See have always — or at least since the 19th century (under Pius IX, Leo XIII, Pius X, Benedict XV, and Pius XI) with its apportioning of Catholicism into quasi-political tendencies — manifested themselves by the politics of episcopal designation which reflected them. But since the Council, this means of governing has acquired considerably greater importance, or rather it has remained practically the sole means for a power without power. Let us remember the effect of the anti-Franco nominations of Pope Paul VI in Spain. In the same way, the almost systematic choice of moderate candidates under John Paul II has recast most of the national bishoprics and the make-up of the College of Cardinals. Pope Benedict's course, in this domain, will be the most difficult to put into operation. Because he must proceed by degrees: for example, the number of French bishops who meet an active Ratzingerian profile is small, that is, men ready to distinguish themselves from their conciliar clergy.

Normally, little by little, men would acquire positions of command or responsibility who not only fully share the views of restorationist documents such as the Instruction of 1997 "on some questions concerning the collaboration of the faithful laity to the priestly ministry" and the Instruction *Redemptoris sacramentum* of 2004 on the extirpation of liturgical abuses, but who also themselves will rely on the support of priests with the same views. This is where we must sketch in one of the decisive elements of the change in course: the opposition of generations in the clergy, between that which "made the Council" and the following one, must enter into another phase.

In France, the second generation — still a minority among clerics, and of indecisive weight among practicing Catholics — is on the way to being legitimized. It is only necessary to see the enthusiastic reactions of the "winners" in contrast to the frankly hostile reactions of the "losers" in the dioceses and convents. Thus, it is not really a matter of one party taking power and replacing the other. Rather it is a new balance of forces establishing itself almost on its own in a worn-out body, the weakening of the conciliar "conservatism" of the diocesan apparatus having been advanced by the disappearance of the clergy, the constant hemorrhage of the faithful and the ever more worrisome financial crisis. "Mission" and "evanglization" are the bywords of the new bishops: fundamentally, it is the teaching of the catechism and Christian preaching in plain language that are and will be the priorities of the "generation of Benedict XVI" which is in the process of forming.

It should be noted that the bishops and priests of this tendency repeat that they want to remain open to "all" in order to advance this pastoral awakening, aiming in fact at those for whom this participation was barred until now: the traditionalists, upon whom they would like to be able to count as an auxiliary force and among whom there are some who are very close. Certainly, this "generation of Benedict XVI" would like to avoid a direct criticism of the "spirit of the Council." Nonetheless, it is led there, *de facto*, in the liturgical arena. Worship, with its visible aspect — socio-supernatural if one may so describe it — ought more than ever to play the role of "(film) developer" that it had in opposite ways — subjective and reactive — during the post-conciliar period. And if it is true that the new liturgy was the transposition in worship of the ecclesiological upset of the event of Vatican II, let it be stated that inversely, the "return to the interior" so dear to Pope Benedict is manifested first of all by the resacralization of the liturgy. So that the Tridentine Mass, substantially more than the cassock, is the banner of the criticism — implict or explicit, to different degrees and under various modalities — of Vatican II, just as the celebration of the new liturgy in a traditional spirit — preferential choice of Eucharistic Prayer I, classic liturgical vestments, incense, Latin chant, etc. — is so much more characteristic than the wearing of an ecclesiastical habit of the tendency that is being affirmed.

This nerve center, that is to say, the liturgical evolution begun long ago in a certain number of parishes (generally urban) and of communities, should be considered with attention. It ties together two elements: on the one hand, an implicit criticism, under the form of the "good interpretation" of the reform of Pope Paul VI, at least as it developed among the grassroots; on the other, a more or less marked desire, depending on the case, of "ecumenism" in the direction of traditionalism, considered as a reservoir of the liturgy of "before;" frequent mixtures of old and new reflect a public in favor of the reintroduction of traditional elements in the new liturgy.

Now, it is evident that the osmosis between Benedict XVI and his faithful supporters — and even the most traditionalist of them — is total on this point. He himself is certain on two points. First, taking into account the "revolutionary" manner in which, according to the present Pope, the reform of Paul VI proceeded, he has always held that the older liturgy could not be considered as abrogated: he therefore considers that it can legitimately claim a recognized place. The more so in that the public celebration of the Tridentine rite in numerous places can only help powerfully to implement the second conviction: the reform of Pope Paul VI not having yielded the hoped-for fruits after thirty-five years of use, it is necessary, gently and patiently, to proceed to a "reform of the reform" which will bring it back in line with the reforms accomplished by Pius XII during the period of the Liturgical Movement.

Thus, in the movement that is unfolding, the liturgical issue is crucial. Everything is pressing the Tridentine advocates and the restorationists — certainly very unequal in their numerical importance — not so much to merge as to establish a common front, not only from the point of view of the liturgy but also from that of the pastoral mission in the dioceses, which are turning into deserts. Assuredly, if in certain places, parishes, or communities, the "reform of the reform" went so far as to offer Catholics attached to the Tridentine rite the possibility of participating in ceremonies consistent with traditional forms, the movement of *transition* would be considerably accelerated. A part of this fleshing out of the liturgical reform (which will not take place everywhere, but will be manifested in a significant way) has been practically achieved: altar facing God, Roman canon, chanting the Kyriale...This not only in the program but in the practice of Benedict XVI. It is insufficient, though: it is the additional step that is important. The most astute of the restorationists know that the most fundamental criticism of the Mass of Paul VI aims at restoring the definition of the Mass as a propitiatory sacrifice. This through a purging of the rite and the prayers. Pope Benedict knows well — but unlike other partisans of the "reform of the reform," he has refrained from speaking about it until now — that from this perspective, the most flagrant deficit of the rite of Bugnini is caused by the suppression of sacrifical prayers of the Offertory, a veritable enormity with regard to the liturgical tradition, both oriental and Latin.

Cutting the ecumenical Gordian knot

This hesitation concerning the most sensitive of the necessary liturgical repairs — even if it appears concretely modest and easy — is linked to the dogmatic-Tridentine cast it would assume. Because even if most claim otherwise, no one is ignorant of the fact that the unease concerning the liturgical reform is in direct relation to the unease concerning the doctrinal reform of the last Council in the domain which could be called ecumenical: the non-acceptance of the liturgical reform overlies, at least implicitly, the non-acceptance of the conciliar reform.

If informed traditional Catholics wanted to summarize, in the manner of theological propositions, the elements that appear unacceptable to them in the considerations of Vatican II, they would search for them in the three texts which contain views that are frankly new regarding the previous dogmatic corpus, issued precisely from a project with an ecumenical objective elaborated by the Secretariat of the Pontifical Council for Promoting Christian Unity: the decree *Unitatis Redintegratio* on ecumenism, the declaration *Nostra Aetate*, on relations of the Church with non-Christian religions, and the declaration *Dignitatis Humanae*, on religious liberty.

Let us note in passing that the tendency found within the "Benedict XVI vogue" to reduce the doctrinal scope of these texts certainly facilitates the criticism but does not resolve the problem that they pose. This problem touches upon the major preoccupation of the Ratzingerians, namely the unity of Catholics themselves which ecumenism divides, whether for some because they reject it or for others because it undermines their adherence to the *Credo*. External ecumenism serves in effect as a mill to process a new way of confessing the Faith, that of "unity in diversity" which undoes the ecclesial bond of Catholics (the Faith, the sense of communion) much more than it unites with those separated from the Catholic Church: the latent schism which afflicts the Church today is manifested first of all by the demand for a pluralist Church. This is to say that the question of the *interpretation* of the ecumenical doctrine promoted by Vatican II matters to internal unity.

This doctrine is, in fact, more considerable than the two other contentious doctrines, interreligious dialogue and religious liberty, which, precisely, are derived from it. Thus, we realize more and more that the problem of relations with non-Christian religions is largely placed in perspective by the confrontation with secularization. Hans Urs von Balthasar has already spoken in this regard of a gradual "reduction of dialogue," Christianity being practically alone in being able to sustain the intellectual clash with modernity. Besides, the problem of relations with non-Christian religions is on the way to being resolved with the declaration *Dominus Jesus* on the unity and salvific universality of Jesus Christ and of the Church, which affirms among other things that the revelation of Jesus Christ is complete and definitive and that is is necessary to make a distinction between the nature of theological faith in Christian truths and belief in other religions (even if n. 22 states "the *sincere respect* [my emphasis] which the Church has for the religions of the world").

As for the problem of religious liberty (replacing the classical notion of civil tolerance which the notion of liberty accords to the public manifestation of error), it comes from traditional ecclesiatical public law totally unknown today. And here again, an eminently Ratzingerian document, the encyclical *Veritatis Splendor*, contains the elements of an interpretation of the conciliar text in referring in n. 44 to the encyclical *Libertas Praestantissimum* of Leo XIII, which underscores the essential submission of human law to natural law.

Ecumenical doctrine remains first and foremost, the whole problem being concentrated around the ecclesiality of separated churches and communities and of the retraction, if this ecclesiality were strictly recognized, of the necessity of a *return* of the separated churches to the Church from which they are removed. In other words, it is the consecration of "unity in diversity" which by contamination disaggregates the body of Catholics. Joseph Ratzinger had notably advanced the reflection on this question by comparing the separated churches to more or less perfect diocesan Churches. Now, strictly speaking, the particular Churches (dioceses or their equivalents) do not have existence nor salvific efficacy except in the bosom of the Catholic body directed by Peter, just as bishops have no mission, in truth, except by belonging to the College of Bishops united with the Pope.

Thus it is in this domain and around this kind of question that we find the theological knot to be severed by the pontificate that has begun. If the liturgical issue is decisive in its domain, this issue is even more critical. In it, certainly, is found the unity of the Church and of the understanding of what She represents in Herself, but also, and more immediately, of the unity of all vital forces of Catholicism, which the drifts and quarrels following Vatican II have rendered anemic and scattered.

Address of
His Holiness Benedict XVI
to the Roman Curia
offering them his
Christmas Greetings

Thursday, 22 December 2005

Your Eminences,
Venerable Brothers in the Episcopate and in the Presbyterate,
Dear Brothers and Sisters,

"*Expergiscere, homo: quia pro te Deus factus est homo* —
Wake up, O man! For your sake God became man" (St.
Augustine, *Sermo*, 185). With the Christmas celebrations now at
hand, I am opening my Meeting with you, dear collaborators of
the Roman Curia, with St. Augustine's invitation to understand
the true meaning of Christ's Birth.

I address to each one my most cordial greeting and I thank you
for the sentiments of devotion and affection, effectively conveyed to
me by your Cardinal Dean, to whom I address my gratitude.

God became man for our sake: this is the message which,
every year, from the silent grotto of Bethlehem spreads even to
the most out-of-the-way corners of the earth. Christmas is a
feast of light and peace, it is a day of inner wonder and joy that

expands throughout the universe, because "God became man." From the humble grotto of Bethlehem, the eternal Son of God, who became a tiny Child, addresses each one of us: he calls us, invites us to be reborn in him so that, with him, we may live eternally in communion with the Most Holy Trinity.

Our hearts brimming with the joy that comes from this knowledge, let us think back to the events of the year that is coming to an end. We have behind us great events which have left a deep mark on the life of the Church. I am thinking first and foremost of the departure of our beloved Holy Father John Paul II, preceded by a long period of suffering and the gradual loss of speech. No Pope has left us such a quantity of texts as he has bequeathed to us; no previous Pope was able to visit the whole world like him and speak directly to people from all the continents.

In the end, however, his lot was a journey of suffering and silence. Unforgettable for us are the images of Palm Sunday when, holding an olive branch and marked by pain, he came to the window and imparted the Lord's Blessing as he himself was about to walk towards the Cross.

Next was the scene in his Private Chapel when, holding the Crucifix, he took part in the Way of the Cross at the Colosseum, where he had so often led the procession carrying the Cross himself.

Lastly came his silent Blessing on Easter Sunday, in which we saw the promise of the Resurrection, of eternal life, shine out through all his suffering. With his words and actions, the Holy Father gave us great things; equally important is the lesson he imparted to us from the chair of suffering and silence.

In his last book *"Memory and Identity"* (Weidenfeld and Nicolson, 2005), he has left us an interpretation of suffering that is not a theological or philosophical theory but a fruit that matured on his personal path of suffering which he walked, sustained by faith in the Crucified Lord. This interpretation, which he worked out in faith and which gave meaning to his suffering lived in communion with that of the Lord, spoke through his silent pain, transforming it into an important message.

Both at the beginning and once again at the end of the book mentioned, the Pope shows that he is deeply touched by the spectacle of the power of evil, which we dramatically experienced in the century that has just ended. He says in his text: "The evil... was not a small-scale evil.... It was an evil of gigantic proportions, an evil which availed itself of state structures in order to accomplish its wicked work, an evil built up into a system" (p. 189).

Might evil be invincible? Is it the ultimate power of history? Because of the experience of evil, for Pope Wojtya the question of redemption became the essential and central question of his life and thought as a Christian. Is there a limit against which the power of evil shatters? "Yes, there is," the Pope replies in this book of his, as well as in his Encyclical on redemption.

The power that imposes a limit on evil is Divine Mercy. Violence, the display of evil, is opposed in history — as "the totally other" of God, God's own power — by Divine Mercy. The Lamb is stronger than the dragon, we could say together with the Book of Revelation.

At the end of the book, in a retrospective review of the attack of 13 May 1981 and on the basis of the experience of his journey with God and with the world, John Paul II further deepened this answer.

What limits the force of evil, the power, in brief, which overcomes it — this is how he says it — is God's suffering, the suffering of the Son of God on the Cross: "The suffering of the Crucified God is not just one form of suffering alongside others.... In sacrificing himself for us all, Christ gave a new meaning to suffering, opening up a new dimension, a new order: the order of love.... The passion of Christ on the Cross gave a radically new meaning to suffering, transforming it from within.... It is this suffering which burns and consumes evil with the flame of love.... All human suffering, all pain, all infirmity contains within itself a promise of salvation;... evil is present in the world partly so as to awaken our love, our self-gift in generous and disinterested service to those visited by suffering.... Christ has redeemed the world: "By his wounds we are healed' (Is 53: 5)" (p. 189, ff.).

All this is not merely learned theology, but the expression of a faith lived and matured through suffering. Of course, we must do all we can to alleviate suffering and prevent the injustice that causes the suffering of the innocent. However, we must also do the utmost to ensure that people can discover the meaning of suffering and are thus able to accept their own suffering and to unite it with the suffering of Christ.

In this way, it is merged with redemptive love and consequently becomes a force against the evil in the world.

The response across the world to the Pope's death was an overwhelming demonstration of gratitude for the fact that in his ministry he offered himself totally to God for the world; a thanksgiving for the fact that in a world full of hatred and violence he taught anew love and suffering in the service of others; he showed us, so to speak, in the flesh, the Redeemer, redemption, and gave us the certainty that indeed, evil does not have the last word in the world.

I would now like to mention, if briefly, another two events also initiated by Pope John Paul II: they are the World Youth Day celebrated in Cologne and the Synod of Bishops on the Eucharist, which also ended the Year of the Eucharist inaugurated by Pope John Paul II.

The World Youth Day has lived on as a great gift in the memory of those present. More than a million young people gathered in the City of Cologne on the Rhine River and in the neighboring towns to listen together to the Word of God, to pray together, to receive the Sacraments of Reconciliation and the Eucharist, to sing and to celebrate together, to rejoice in life and to worship and receive the Lord in the Eucharist during the great meetings on Saturday evening and Sunday. Joy simply reigned throughout those days.

Apart from keeping order, the police had nothing to do — the Lord had gathered his family, tangibly overcoming every frontier and barrier, and in the great communion between us, he made us experience his presence.

The motto chosen for those days — "We have come to worship him!", contained two great images which encouraged the right approach from the outset. First there was the image of the pilgrimage, the image of the person who, looking beyond his own affairs and daily life, sets out in search of his essential destination, the truth, the right life, God.

This image of the person on his way towards the goal of life contained another two clear indications.

First of all, there was the invitation not to see the world that surrounds us solely as raw material with which we can do something, but to try to discover in it "the Creator's handwriting," the creative reason and the love from which the world was born and of which the universe speaks to us, if we pay attention, if our inner senses awaken and acquire perception of the deepest dimensions of reality.

As a second element there is a further invitation: to listen to the historical revelation which alone can offer us the key to the interpretation of the silent mystery of creation, pointing out to us the practical way towards the true Lord of the world and of history, who conceals himself in the poverty of the stable in Bethlehem.

The other image contained in the World Youth Day motto was the person worshipping: "We have come to worship him." Before any activity, before the world can change there must be worship. Worship alone sets us truly free; worship alone gives us the criteria for our action. Precisely in a world in which guiding criteria are absent and the threat exists that each person will be a law unto himself, it is fundamentally necessary to stress worship.

For all those who were present the intense silence of that million young people remains unforgettable, a silence that united and uplifted us all when the Lord in the Blessed Sacrament was placed on the altar. Let us cherish in our hearts the images of Cologne: they are signs that continue to be valid. Without mentioning individual names, I would like on this occasion to thank everyone who made World Youth Day possible; but especially, let us together thank the Lord, for indeed, he alone could give us those days in the way in which we lived them.

The word "adoration" [worship] brings us to the second great event that I wish to talk about: the Synod of Bishops and the Year of the Eucharist. Pope John Paul II, with the Encyclical *Ecclesia de Eucharistia* and the Apostolic Letter *Mane Nobiscum Domine*, gave us the essential clues and at the same time, with his personal experience of Eucharistic faith, put the Church's teaching into practice.

Moreover, the Congregation for Divine Worship, in close connection with the Encyclical, published the Instruction *Redemptionis Sacramentum* as a practical guide to the correct implementation of the conciliar Constitution on the liturgy and liturgical reform. In addition to all this, was it really possible to say anything new, to develop further the whole of this teaching?

This was exactly the great experience of the Synod, during which a reflection of the riches of the Eucharistic life of the Church today and the inexhaustibility of her Eucharistic faith could be perceived in the Fathers' contributions. What the Fathers thought and expressed must be presented, in close connection with the *Propositiones* of the Synod, in a Post-Synodal Document.

Here, once again, I only wish to underline that point which a little while ago we already mentioned in the context of World Youth Day: adoration of the Risen Lord, present in the Eucharist with flesh and blood, with body and soul, with divinity and humanity.

It is moving for me to see how everywhere in the Church the joy of Eucharistic adoration is reawakening and being fruitful. In the period of liturgical reform, Mass and adoration outside it were often seen as in opposition to one another: it was thought that the Eucharistic Bread had not been given to us to be contemplated, but to be eaten, as a widespread objection claimed at that time.

The experience of the prayer of the Church has already shown how nonsensical this antithesis was. Augustine had formerly said: *"...nemo autem illam carnem manducat, nisi prius adoraverit;... peccemus non adorando* — No one should eat this flesh without first adoring it;... we should sin were we not to adore it" (cf. Enarr. in Ps 98: 9 CCL XXXIX 1385).

Indeed, we do not merely receive something in the Eucharist. It is the encounter and unification of persons; the person, however, who comes to meet us and desires to unite himself to us is the Son of God. Such unification can only be brought about by means of adoration.

Receiving the Eucharist means adoring the One whom we receive. Precisely in this way and only in this way do we become one with him. Therefore, the development of Eucharistic adoration, as it took shape during the Middle Ages, was the most consistent consequence of the Eucharistic mystery itself: only in adoration can profound and true acceptance develop. And it is precisely this personal act of encounter with the Lord that develops the social mission which is contained in the Eucharist and desires to break down barriers, not only the barriers between the Lord and us but also and above all those that separate us from one another.

The last event of this year on which I wish to reflect here is the celebration of the conclusion of the Second Vatican Council 40 years ago. This memory prompts the question: What has been the result of the Council? Was it well received? What, in the acceptance of the Council, was good and what was inadequate or mistaken? What still remains to be done? No one can deny that in vast areas of the Church the implementation of the Council has been somewhat difficult, even without wishing to apply to what occurred in these years the description that St. Basil, the great Doctor of the Church, made of the Church's situation after the Council of Nicea: he compares her situation to a naval battle in the darkness of the storm, saying among other things: "The raucous shouting of those who through disagreement rise up against one another, the incomprehensible chatter, the confused din of uninterrupted clamoring, has now filled almost the whole of the Church, falsifying through excess or failure the right doctrine of the faith..." (*De Spiritu Sancto*, XXX, 77; PG 32, 213 A; SCh 17 ff., p. 524).

We do not want to apply precisely this dramatic description to the situation of the post-conciliar period, yet something from all that occurred is nevertheless reflected in it. The question arises: Why has the implementation of the Council, in large parts of the Church, thus far been so difficult?

Well, it all depends on the correct interpretation of the Council or — as we would say today — on its proper hermeneutics, the correct key to its interpretation and application. The problems in its implementation arose from the fact that two contrary hermeneutics came face to face and quarrelled with each other. One caused confusion, the other, silently but more and more visibly, bore and is bearing fruit.

On the one hand, there is an interpretation that I would call "a hermeneutic of discontinuity and rupture;" it has frequently availed itself of the sympathies of the mass media, and also one trend of modern theology. On the other, there is the "hermeneutic of reform," of renewal in the continuity of the one subject-Church which the Lord has given to us. She is a subject which increases in time and develops, yet always remaining the same, the one subject of the journeying People of God.

The hermeneutic of discontinuity risks ending in a split

between the pre-conciliar Church and the post-conciliar Church. It asserts that the texts of the Council as such do not yet express the true spirit of the Council. It claims that they are the result of compromises in which, to reach unanimity, it was found necessary to keep and reconfirm many old things that are now pointless. However, the true spirit of the Council is not to be found in these compromises but instead in the impulses toward the new that are contained in the texts.

These innovations alone were supposed to represent the true spirit of the Council, and starting from and in conformity with them, it would be possible to move ahead. Precisely because the texts would only imperfectly reflect the true spirit of the Council and its newness, it would be necessary to go courageously beyond the texts and make room for the newness in which the Council's deepest intention would be expressed, even if it were still vague.

In a word: it would be necessary not to follow the texts of the Council but its spirit. In this way, obviously, a vast margin was left open for the question on how this spirit should subsequently be defined and room was consequently made for every whim.

The nature of a Council as such is therefore basically misunderstood. In this way, it is considered as a sort of constituent that eliminates an old constitution and creates a new one. However, the Constituent Assembly needs a mandator and then confirmation by the mandator, in other words, the people the constitution must serve. The Fathers had no such mandate and no one had ever given them one; nor could anyone have given them one because the essential constitution of the Church comes from the Lord and was given to us so that we might attain eternal life and, starting from this perspective, be able to illuminate life in time and time itself.

Through the Sacrament they have received, Bishops are stewards of the Lord's gift. They are "stewards of the mysteries of God" (I Cor 4: 1); as such, they must be found to be "faithful" and "wise" (cf. Lk 12: 41-48). This requires them to administer the Lord's gift in the right way, so that it is not left concealed in some hiding place but bears fruit, and the Lord may end by saying to the administrator: "Since you were dependable in a small matter I will put you in charge of larger affairs" (cf. Mt 25: 14-30; Lk 19: 11-27).

These Gospel parables express the dynamic of fidelity required in the Lord's service; and through them it becomes clear that, as in a Council, the dynamic and fidelity must converge.

The hermeneutic of discontinuity is countered by the hermeneutic of reform, as it was presented first by Pope John XXIII in his Speech inaugurating the Council on 11 October 1962 and later by Pope Paul VI in his Discourse for the Council's conclusion on 7 December 1965.

Here I shall cite only John XXIII's well-known words, which unequivocally express this hermeneutic when he says that the Council wishes "to transmit the doctrine, pure and integral, without any attenuation or distortion." And he continues: "Our duty is not only to guard this precious treasure, as if we were concerned only with antiquity, but to dedicate ourselves with an earnest will and without fear to that work which our era demands of us. ..." It is necessary that "adherence to all the teaching of the Church in its entirety and preciseness..." be presented in "faithful and perfect conformity to the authentic doctrine, which, however, should be studied and expounded through the methods of research and through the literary forms of modern thought. The substance of the ancient doctrine of the deposit of faith is one thing, and the way in which it is presented is another...", retaining the same meaning and message (*The Documents of Vatican II*, Walter M. Abbott, S.J., p. 715).

It is clear that this commitment to expressing a specific truth in a new way demands new thinking on this truth and a new and vital relationship with it; it is also clear that new words can only develop if they come from an informed understanding of the truth expressed, and on the other hand, that a reflection on faith also requires that this faith be lived. In this regard, the program that Pope John XXIII proposed was extremely demanding, indeed, just as the synthesis of fidelity and dynamic is demanding.

However, wherever this interpretation guided the implementation of the Council, new life developed and new fruit ripened. Forty years after the Council, we can show that the positive is far greater and livelier than it appeared to be in the turbulent years around 1968. Today, we see that although the good seed developed slowly, it is nonetheless growing; and our deep gratitude for the work done by the Council is likewise growing.

In his Discourse closing the Council, Paul VI pointed out a further specific reason why a hermeneutic of discontinuity can seem convincing.

In the great dispute about man which marks the modern epoch, the Council had to focus in particular on the theme of anthropology. It had to question the relationship between the Church and her faith on the one hand, and man and the contemporary world on the other (cf. ibid.). The question becomes even clearer if, instead of the generic term "contemporary world," we opt for another that is more precise: the Council had to determine in a new way the relationship between the Church and the modern era.

This relationship had a somewhat stormy beginning with the Galileo case. It was then totally interrupted when Kant described "religion within pure reason" and when, in the radical phase of the French Revolution, an image of the State and the human being that practically no longer wanted to allow the Church any room was disseminated.

In the 19th century under Pius IX, the clash between the Church's faith and a radical liberalism and the natural sciences, which also claimed to embrace with their knowledge the whole of reality to its limit, stubbornly proposing to make the "hypothesis of God" superfluous, had elicited from the Church a bitter and radical condemnation of this spirit of the modern age. Thus, it seemed that there was no longer any milieu open to a positive and fruitful understanding, and the rejection by those who felt they were the representatives of the modern era was also drastic.

In the meantime, however, the modern age had also experienced developments. People came to realize that the American Revolution was offering a model of a modern State that differed from the theoretical model with radical tendencies that had emerged during the second phase of the French Revolution.

The natural sciences were beginning to reflect more and more clearly their own limitations imposed by their own method, which, despite achieving great things, was nevertheless unable to grasp the global nature of reality.

So it was that both parties were gradually beginning to open up to each other. In the period between the two World Wars and especially after the Second World War, Catholic statesmen demonstrated that a modern secular State could exist that was not neutral regarding values but alive, drawing from the great ethical sources opened by Christianity.

Catholic social doctrine, as it gradually developed, became an important model between radical liberalism and the Marxist theory of the State. The natural sciences, which without reservation professed a method of their own to which God was barred access, realized ever more clearly that this method did not include the whole of reality. Hence, they once again opened their doors to God, knowing that reality is greater than the naturalistic method and all that it can encompass.

It might be said that three circles of questions had formed which then, at the time of the Second Vatican Council, were expecting an answer. First of all, the relationship between faith and modern science had to be redefined. Furthermore, this did not only concern the natural sciences but also historical science for, in a certain school, the historical-critical method claimed to have the last word on the interpretation of the Bible and, demanding total exclusivity for its interpretation of Sacred Scripture, was opposed to important points in the interpretation elaborated by the faith of the Church.

Secondly, it was necessary to give a new definition to the relationship between the Church and the modern State that would make room impartially for citizens of various religions and ideologies, merely assuming responsibility for an orderly and tolerant coexistence among them and for the freedom to practice their own religion.

Thirdly, linked more generally to this was the problem of religious tolerance — a question that required a new definition of the relationship between the Christian faith and the world religions. In particular, before the recent crimes of the Nazi regime and, in general, with a retrospective look at a long and difficult history, it was necessary to evaluate and define in a new way the relationship between the Church and the faith of Israel.

These are all subjects of great importance — they were the great themes of the second part of the Council — on which it is impossible to reflect more broadly in this context. It is clear that in all these sectors, which all together form a single problem, some kind of discontinuity might emerge. Indeed, a discontinuity had been revealed but in which, after the various distinctions between concrete historical situations and their requirements had been made, the continuity of principles proved not to have been abandoned. It is easy to miss this fact at a first glance.

It is precisely in this combination of continuity and discontinuity at different levels that the very nature of true reform consists. In this process of innovation in continuity we must learn to understand more practically than before that the Church's decisions on contingent matters — for example, certain practical forms of liberalism or a free interpretation of the Bible — should necessarily be contingent themselves, precisely because they refer to a specific reality that is changeable in itself. It was necessary to learn to recognize that in these decisions it is only the principles that express the permanent aspect, since they remain as an undercurrent, motivating decisions from within.

On the other hand, not so permanent are the practical forms that depend on the historical situation and are therefore subject to change.

Basic decisions, therefore, continue to be well-grounded, whereas the way they are applied to new contexts can change. Thus, for example, if religious freedom were to be considered an expression of the human inability to discover the truth and thus become a canonization of relativism, then this social and historical necessity is raised inappropriately to the metaphysical level and thus stripped of its true meaning. Consequently, it cannot be accepted by those who believe that the human person is capable of knowing the truth about God and, on the basis of the inner dignity of the truth, is bound to this knowledge.

It is quite different, on the other hand, to perceive religious freedom as a need that derives from human coexistence, or indeed, as an intrinsic consequence of the truth that cannot be externally imposed but that the person must adopt only through the process of conviction.

The Second Vatican Council, recognizing and making its own an essential principle of the modern State with the Decree on Religious Freedom, has recovered the deepest patrimony of the Church. By so doing she can be conscious of being in full harmony with the teaching of Jesus himself (cf. Mt 22: 21), as well as with the Church of the martyrs of all time. The ancient Church naturally prayed for the emperors and political leaders out of duty (cf. I Tm 2: 2); but while she prayed for the emperors, she refused to worship them and thereby clearly rejected the religion of the State.

The martyrs of the early Church died for their faith in that God who was revealed in Jesus Christ, and for this very reason they also died for freedom of conscience and the freedom to profess one's own faith — a profession that no State can impose but which, instead, can only be claimed with God's grace in freedom of conscience. A missionary Church known for proclaiming her message to all peoples must necessarily work for the freedom of the faith. She desires to transmit the gift of the truth that exists for one and all.

At the same time, she assures peoples and their Governments that she does not wish to destroy their identity and culture by doing so, but to give them, on the contrary, a response which, in their innermost depths, they are waiting for — a response with which the multiplicity of cultures is not lost but instead unity between men and women increases and thus also peace between peoples.

The Second Vatican Council, with its new definition of the relationship between the faith of the Church and certain essential elements of modern thought, has reviewed or even corrected certain historical decisions, but in this apparent discontinuity it has actually preserved and deepened her inmost nature and true identity.

The Church, both before and after the Council, was and is the same Church, one, holy, catholic and apostolic, journeying on through time; she continues "her pilgrimage amid the persecutions of the world and the consolations of God," proclaiming the death of the Lord until he comes (cf. *Lumen Gentium*, n. 8).

Those who expected that with this fundamental "yes" to the modern era all tensions would be dispelled and that the "openness towards the world" accordingly achieved would transform everything into pure harmony, had underestimated the inner tensions as well as the contradictions inherent in the modern epoch.

They had underestimated the perilous frailty of human nature which has been a threat to human progress in all the periods of history and in every historical constellation. These dangers, with the new possibilities and new power of man over matter and over himself, did not disappear but instead acquired new dimensions: a look at the history of the present day shows this clearly.

In our time too, the Church remains a "sign that will be opposed" (Lk 2: 34) — not without reason did Pope John Paul II, then still a Cardinal, give this title to the theme for the Spiritual Exercises he preached in 1976 to Pope Paul VI and the Roman Curia. The Council could not have intended to abolish the Gospel's opposition to human dangers and errors.

On the contrary, it was certainly the Council's intention to overcome erroneous or superfluous contradictions in order to present to our world the requirement of the Gospel in its full greatness and purity.

The steps the Council took towards the modern era which had rather vaguely been presented as "openness to the world," belong in short to the perennial problem of the relationship between faith and reason that is re-emerging in ever new forms. The situation that the Council had to face can certainly be compared to events of previous epochs.

In his First Letter, St. Peter urged Christians always to be ready to give an answer (*apo-logia*) to anyone who asked them for the logos, the reason for their faith (cf. 3: 15).

This meant that biblical faith had to be discussed and come into contact with Greek culture and learn to recognize through interpretation the separating line but also the convergence and the affinity between them in the one reason, given by God.

When, in the 13th century through the Jewish and Arab philosophers, Aristotelian thought came into contact with Medieval Christianity formed in the Platonic tradition and faith and reason risked entering an irreconcilable contradiction, it was above all St. Thomas Aquinas who mediated the new encounter between faith and Aristotelian philosophy, thereby setting faith in a positive relationship with the form of reason prevalent in his time. There is no doubt that the wearing dispute between modern reason and the Christian faith, which had begun negatively with the Galileo case, went through many phases, but with the Second Vatican Council the time came when broad new thinking was required.

Its content was certainly only roughly traced in the conciliar texts, but this determined its essential direction, so that the dialogue between reason and faith, particularly important today, found its bearings on the basis of the Second Vatican Council.

This dialogue must now be developed with great open-mindedness but also with that clear discernment that the world rightly expects of us in this very moment. Thus, today we can look with gratitude at the Second Vatican Council: if we interpret and implement it guided by a right hermeneutic, it can be and can become increasingly powerful for the ever necessary renewal of the Church.

Lastly, should I perhaps recall once again that 19 April this year on which, to my great surprise, the College of Cardinals elected me as the Successor of Pope John Paul II, as a Successor of St. Peter on the chair of the Bishop of Rome? Such an office was far beyond anything I could ever have imagined as my vocation. It was, therefore, only with a great act of trust in God that I was able to say in obedience my "yes" to this choice. Now as then, I also ask you all for your prayer, on whose power and support I rely.

At the same time, I would like to warmly thank all those who have welcomed me and still welcome me with great trust, goodness and understanding, accompanying me day after day with their prayers.

Christmas is now at hand. The Lord God did not counter the threats of history with external power, as we human beings would expect according to the prospects of our world. His weapon is goodness. He revealed himself as a child, born in a stable. This is precisely how he counters with his power, completely different from the destructive powers of violence. In this very way he saves us. In this very way he shows us what saves.

In these days of Christmas, let us go to meet him full of trust, like the shepherds, like the Wise Men of the East. Let us ask Mary to lead us to the Lord. Let us ask him himself to make his face shine upon us. Let us ask him also to defeat the violence in the world and to make us experience the power of his goodness. With these sentiments, I warmly impart to you all my Apostolic Blessing.

Cardinal Ratzinger's 1988 Remarks to the Bishops of Chile and Colombia

Address of Joseph Cardinal Ratizinger, Prefect of the Congregation for the Doctrine of the Faith, to the Bishops of Chile and Colombia as reported by the Spanish edition of L'Osservatore Romano on August 7 1988. This address was delivered in Santiago, Chile on July 13 1988 and in Bogota on July 15th.

Respected and dear brothers:

First and foremost I would like to express my cordial gratitude for your very kind invitation to visit your country and for providing me with this occasion to meet you and to engage in a fraternal dialogue. It is not possible to know a country in a visit of some short days, nevertheless it is very important for me to have a chance to see the places where you work and to have in some ways an experience of the environment of the life of the Church in this land.

The objective of my words is to strengthen the dialogue that we want to share. In a general way, normally I use these meetings to present briefly some of the most important questions that are considered by the Congregation. Nevertheless the schism that seems to be opening with the bishops' ordinations of June 30th leads me to put aside for this time this custom. Today I would simply like to comment on some things about the case concerning Msgr. Lefebvre. More than talking in depth on what has happened, it seems to me that it is more important to value the teachings that the Church can apply today and for the future. For that I would like to anticipate in the first place some observations on the attitude of the Holy See in the talks with Msgr. Lefebvre and then continue with a reflection on the general causes that caused the situation over and above this particular case are a concern for all of us.

1. The attitude of the Holy See in the talks with Lefebvre

In recent months we have invested a lot of work in the problem of Lefebvre, with the sincere intention of creating for his movement an adequate vital space within the Church. From different sides the Holy See has been criticized for this. It has been said that we have yielded to the pressure of a schism, that we have not defended the Second Vatican Council with sufficient energy; that we acted with great severity with the progressive movements even as we displayed too much understanding of the traditionalist rebellion. The development of events is enough to disprove these assertions. The mythical harshness of the Vatican so dear to the progressives has proven to be mere empty words. Until now, in fact, basically only warnings have been published; in no case have there been canonical penalties in the strict sense. And the fact that Lefebvre denounced an agreement that had already been signed, shows that the Holy See, while it made truly generous concessions, did not grant him that complete license which he desired. Lefebvre has recognized that he had to accept Vatican II and the affirmations of the post-conciliar Magisterium, according to the proper authority of each document. There is a glaring contradiction in the fact that it is just the people who have let no occasion slip to let the world know of their disobedience to the Pope, and to the magisterial declarations of the last 20 years, who think that they have the right to judge that this attitude is too mild and demand an absolute obedience to Vatican II. In a similar way they would claim that the Vatican has conceded a right to dissent to Lefebvre which has been persistently denied to the promoters of a progressive tendency. In reality, the only point which is affirmed in the agreement, following *Lumen Gentium* 25, is the plain fact that not all documents of the Council have the same rank. For the rest, it was explicitly laid down in the text that was signed [by Msgr. Lefebvre] that public polemics must be avoided, and an attitude was required of positive respect for official decisions and declarations. It was conceded, in addition, that the Fraternity of St. Pius X would be able to present to the Holy See — which reserves to itself the sole right of decision — their particular difficulties in regard to interpretations of juridical and liturgical reforms. All of this shows plainly that in this difficult dialogue Rome has united generosity, in all that was negotiable, with firmness in essentials. The explanation which Msgr. Lefebvre has given, for the retraction of his agreement, is revealing. He declared that he in the end understood that the agreement he signed aimed only at integrating his foundation into the "Conciliar Church." The Catholic Church in union with the Pope is, according to him, the "Conciliar Church" which has broken with its own past. It seems indeed that he is no longer able to see that we are dealing with the Catholic Church in the totality of its Tradition, and that Vatican II belongs to that.

2. Reflection on the deepest causes of the Lefebvre case

Without any doubt, the problem that Lefebvre has posed has not been concluded by the rupture of June 30th. It would be too simple to take refuge in a sort of triumphalism, and to think that this difficulty has ceased to exist from the moment in which the movement led by Lefebvre has separated itself by a clean break with the Church. A Christian never can, or should, take pleasure in a rupture. Even though it is absolutely certain the fault cannot be attributed to the Holy See, it is a duty for us to examine ourselves, as to what errors we have made, and which ones we are making even now. The criteria with which we judge the past in the Vatican II decree on ecumenism must be used — as is logical — to judge the present as well. One of the basic discoveries of the theology of ecumenism is that schisms can take place only when certain truths and certain values of the Christian faith are no longer lived and loved within the Church. The truth which is marginalized becomes autonomous, remains detached from the whole of the ecclesiastical structure, and a new movement then forms itself around it. We must reflect on this fact: that a large number of Catholics, far beyond the narrow circle of the Fraternity of Lefebvre, see this man as a guide, in some sense, or at least as a useful teacher. It will not do to attribute everything to political motives, to nostalgia, or to cultural factors of minor importance. These causes do not explain the attraction which is felt especially by the young, who come from many different nations, and who are surrounded by completely different political and cultural realities. Indeed one can take a narrow view; nevertheless this situation as a whole would be unthinkable unless there were good elements at work here which in general do not find sufficient vital space in today's Church. For those reasons, we ought to see this matter primarily as the occasion for an examination of conscience. We should allow ourselves to ask fundamental questions about the defects in the pastoral life of the Church which are exposed by these events. Thus we will be able to offer a place within the Church to those who are seeking and demanding it, and succeed in destroying all reason for schism. We can make such schism pointless by renewing the interior realities of the Church. There are three points, I think, that it is important to think about.

a. The sacred and the profane

There are many motives that might have led a great number of people to seek a refuge in the traditional liturgy. The first and very important one is that they find the dignity of the sacred preserved there. After the Council there were many who deliberately raised "desacralization" to the level of a program, on the plea that the New Testament abolished the cult of the Temple: the veil of the Temple which was torn from top to bottom at the moment of Christ's death on the Cross is, according to certain people, the sign of the end of the sacred. The death of Jesus, outside the City walls — that is to say — in the public world, is now the true religion. Worship, if it exists at all, should be found in the non-sacredness of daily life, in love that is lived. Inspired by such reasoning, they put aside the sacred vestments; they have despoiled the churches as much as they could of that splendor which brings to mind the sacred; and they have reduced the liturgy to the language and the gestures of ordinary life, by means of greetings, common signs of friendship, and similar things.

There is no doubt that, with those theories and practices of that sort, they have entirely disregarded the true connection between the Old and the New Testaments: It is forgotten that this world is not yet the Kingdom of God, and that the "Holy One of God" (John 6:69) continues to exist in contradiction to this world; that we have need of purification before we draw near to Him; that the profane, even after the death and the Resurrection of Jesus, has not become "the holy." The Risen One has appeared, only to those whose heart has been opened to Him, to the Holy; He did not manifest Himself to all the World. It is in this way a new space has been opened for worship to which all of us would now submit; this worship which consists in drawing near to the community of the Risen One, at whose feet the women prostrated themselves and adored Him. I do not want to develop this point any further now; I confine myself to coming straight to this conclusion: we ought to recover the dimension of the sacred in the liturgy. The liturgy is not a festivity; it is not a meeting for the purpose of having a good time. It is of no importance that the pastor has come up with suggestive ideas or imaginative novelties. In the liturgy the Thrice-Holy God becomes present amongst us; it is the burning bush; it is the Alliance of God with man in Jesus Christ, who has died and risen again. The grandeur of the liturgy does not rest upon the fact that it offers interesting entertainment, but that the Totally Other touches us, whom we are not capable of summoning. He comes because He wills it. In other words, the essential in the liturgy is the mystery, which is realized in the common ritual of the Church; all the rest diminishes it. Men experiment with it in lively fashion, and find themselves deceived when the mystery is transformed into a form of entertainment, when the chief actor in the liturgy is not the Living God but the priest or the liturgical director.

b. The Faith and its continuity

To defend Vatican II, against Msgr. Lefebvre, as valid and binding for the Church is and will continue to be a necessity. Nevertheless, there is a narrow-minded attitude that isolates the Council, and that has caused opposition. Many interpretations give the impression that, from Vatican II onward, everything has been changed, and that what preceded it has no value or, at best, has value only in the light of Vatican II. The Second Vatican Council is not treated as a part of the entire living Tradition of the Church, but as an end of Tradition, a new start from zero.

The truth is that this particular Council has not defined any dogma at all, and it deliberately chose to remain on a modest level, as a merely pastoral council; and yet many treat it as though it had made itself into a sort of superdogma which takes away the importance of all the rest.

This idea is especially reinforced by things that happen daily. That which previously was considered most holy — the form in which the liturgy was handed down — suddenly appears as the most forbidden of all things, and the one thing that can certainly be rejected. It is considered intolerable to criticize decisions which have been taken since the Council; on the other hand, when ancient rules are put in question, or even of the great truths of the Faith — for instance, the corporal virginity of Mary, the bodily resurrection of Jesus, the immortality of the soul, etc. — there is either no reaction at all or reaction only comes with the greatest moderation. I myself, when I was a professor, have seen how the very same bishop who, before the Council, had refused another professor who was really irreproachable, for a certain crudeness of speech, was not prepared, after the Council, to dismiss a professor who openly denied certain fundamental truths of the Faith. All of this leads a great number of people to ask themselves if the Church of today is really the same as that of yesterday, or if they have changed it for something else without telling the people.

The only way in which Vatican II can be made credible is to present it as it is; as a part of the unbroken and unique Tradition of the Church and of her faith.

c. The unicity of the Truth

Putting aside the liturgical question, the central points of the conflict [with the traditionalists] are the attack on the Decree on Religious Liberty and the so called spirit of Assisi. In those matters Lefebvre draws the boundary between his position and the Catholic Church of our days. It is not necessary to add expressly that we cannot accept his views in those matters. But we are not going to deal here with his mistakes. We want to ask ourselves where is our lack of clarity. For Lefebvre it is the question of the struggle against liberal ideology and against making the truth relative. It is evident that we are not in agreement with him that the text of the Council on religious liberty and the prayer of Assisi (in accordance with the willed intentions of the Pope) lead to relativism.

Nevertheless, it is true that in the spiritual movement of the post-conciliar era, many times the truth was either forgotten or suppressed; here perhaps we confront the crucial problem for theology and for pastoral work today. The "truth" was said to be a claim that is too exalted, a "triumphalism" that cannot be permitted any longer. This turn of mind has been illustrated clearly in the crisis that affects the missionary ideal and its practice. If we do not point to the truth in announcing our faith, and if this truth is no longer essential for the salvation of Man, then the missions lose their meaning. In effect the conclusion has been drawn, and it has been drawn today, that in the future we need only seek for Christians to be good Christians, Moslems good Moslems, Hindus good Hindus, and so forth. If it comes to that, how are we to know when one is a "good" Christian, or a "good" Moslem? The idea that all religions are — if you talk seriously — only symbols of what ultimately is incomprehensible is rapidly gaining ground in theology, and has already penetrated into liturgical practice. When things get to this point, faith as such is abandoned, because faith really consists in the fact that I am committing myself to the truth as far as it is known. So in this matter also we have every motive to return to the right path. If once again we succeed in pointing out and living the fullness of the Catholic religion with regard to these points, we may hope that the schism of Lefebvre will not be of long duration.

NOTES

1. To the degree that one intends by this term not the deposit presented once and for all to the Apostles — the "constitutive deposit," as the theologians call it — but "living" clarification of this deposit throughout the history of the Church. In other words, it is not the Deposit of Faith that evolves, but rather the clarification of this deposit that lives and develops.

2. *Commonitorium* 1, c. 23

3. Or no longer dares. The Apostolic Letter *Ordinatio Sacerdotalis* of May 22, 1994, is the post-conciliar document that most seems to approach an infallible act of the Magisterium. Now, on October 28, 1995, the Congregation for the Doctrine of the Faith stipulated that the act was not such in itself: "In the present case, an act of the ordinary pontifical Magisterium, in itself non-infallible, attests to the infallible character of the teaching of a doctrine already in possession of the Church."

4. The new liturgy needs "instructions," said Michel Gitton, in presenting his book, *Initiation à la liturgie romaine (Initiation of the Roman Liturgy*, Ad Solem, 2003), a manifesto in favor of the most traditional possible interpretation.

5. In truth, if the principle of female ordination were officially adopted, there would be few actual feminine vocations, but it is the fact of the "segregation" represented by the prohibition that is incomprehensible to the modern mind generally, and thus, to a good portion of Catholics.

6. See Chapter V.

7. "Similarly excluded is any action which either before, at the moment of, or after sexual intercourse, is specifically intended to prevent procreation — whether as an end or as a means."

8. *La Grande Peur des biens-pensants — Essais et écrits de combat I (The Great Fear of the Right Thinkers — Essays and Writings of Combat I)*, Gallimard, Bibliothèque de la Pléiade, 1971, p.345.

9. The encyclical of Pope Leo XIII, *Au milieu des sollicitudes (In the Midst of Solicitudes)*, of February 16, 1892, and the radio message of Pope Pius XII on December 24, 1944, on democracy, are isolated rallying cries in the midst of a massively anti-modern Magisterium. The radio message of Pius XII is, in fact, an attempt at recovery of the concept, because it deals with "a healthy democracy founded on the immutable principles of natural law and revealed truths," in other words of a communal democracy of the fourteenth century, but not that of the States he confronted in 1944.

10. "La proposition de foi dans la société actuelle" (The Proposal of Faith in Present-day Society), *La Documentation catholique*, December 4, 1994, p. 1057.

11. "The Church values the democratic system inasmuch as it ensures the participation of citizens in making political choices, guarantees to the governed the possibility both of electing and holding accountable those who govern them, and of replacing them through peaceful means when appropriate." *Centesimus Annus*, n. 46.; more cautiously, *Gaudium et Spes*, n. 31: "Praise is due to those national procedures which allow the largest possible number of citizens to participate in public affairs with genuine freedom."

12. "L'ultra-modernité sonne-t-elle la fin de l'œcuménisme?" ("Does Ultra-modernity Ring the Deathknoll of Ecumenism?"), *Recherches de Science religieuse*, April-June 2001, pp. 177-204

13. Interview which appeared in the Austrian weekly, Die Furche, January 22, 2001, broadly disseminated afterwards.

14. 1991: *The Reception of Vatican II in a local Church. The Example of Synodal Practice of the Church of Quebec, 1920-1987.*

15. Cerf, April 2001

16. Apic, March 3, 2004

17. It constitutes notably an ultra-liberal line from the moral and pastoral point of view. See, for example, the document published by Msgr. Garnier, Archbishop of Cambrai, April 5, 2003 *(L'Eglise de Cambrai,* April 2003), on pastoral care of remarried divorcés: conditions of access to Communion; ceremony at the moment of the "remarriage." Similarly, *Roads of Hope (Chemins d'espérance)*, files published by Msgr. Papin, Bishop of Nancy (2003). And again, *Orientations pour une pastorale des personnes divorcées et divorcées remariées (Guidance for the Counseling of Divorced Persons and the Divorced and Remarried)*, issued by Msgr. Doré, Archbishop of Strasbourg, La Documentation catholique, July 18, 2004, pp. 693-695. Also, the provocative book, *L'Eglise et l'art d'avant-garde (The Church and Avant-garde Art)*, Albin Michel, 2002, containing the interventions of Msgr. Rouet, Bishop of Poitiers, and of Msgr. Louis, Bishop of Châlons.

18. It is, like the opposite tendency, extremely diverse, including quasi-traditionalists, mystics, prudent administrators, charismatics, and others, not to mention unclassifiable individuals or groups. Regarding the high officials of the Church, in Chapter VI, I will distinguish within the center-right a restorationist tendency which is fairly close to the traditional world, and a tendency among compromisers toward the preservation of the conciliar acquisitions.

19. The diocesan Synods of the past two decades have been, in this regard, a privileged point of transaction between the aspirations toward modernity and the demand of fidelity to the source (see especially the collective work *Le gouvernement de l'Eglise catholique. Synodes et exercice du pouvoir (The Government of the Catholic Church. Synods and the Exercise of Power)*, edited by Jacques Palard, Cerf, 1997).

20. Are they still laymen? "Undoubtedly the answer to this question cannot be clear and unequivocal," writes Bernard Sesboüé, *N'ayez pas peur! Regard sur l'Église et les ministères aujourd'hui (Be Not Afraid: A Look at the Church and its Ministers Today)*, Desclée de Brouwer, 1996, p.150). One sometimes observes the performance of sacerdotal acts by certain of those persons who are in charge of hospital chaplaincies and to whom it would fall to respond in some way to the requests for Sacraments of Anointing and for Confession, which is clearly lacking any dogmatic basis.

21. N. 23 § 6 of the Apostolic Exhortation *Christifideles Laici* cautioned against "the risk of creating an ecclesial service structure, parallel to that which is founded on the Sacrament of Holy Orders." In the hypothesis presented here, this service structure would henceforth be founded on this Sacrament.

22. *N'ayez pas peur!, op. cit.*, p. 107.

23. *Le Monde*, January 4, 1994; an identical declaration at the BBC, London, on March 12, 1995.

24. André Haquin and Philippe Weber, eds., *Diaconat, XXIe Siècle,* Lumen Vitae/Cerf, 1997, p. 228.

25. *La Documentation catholique*, December 7, 1997, pp. 1009-1020.

26. Michel Scouarnec, *Présider l'assemblée du Christ. Peut-on se passer de prêtres (Presiding over the Assembly of Christ. Can We Do Without Priests)*, L'Atelier, 1996, p. 207.

27. Henri Denis, *Femmes et prêtres mariés dans la société d'aujourd'hui (Women and Married Priests in the Society of Today)*, Karthala, pp. 219-222.

28. Jean Rigal, *L'Eglise en chantier (The Church Under Construction)*, Cerf, 1994, p. 132

29. Interview that appeared in *Il Regno-attualità*, February 1998.

30. Conference organized by priests and laymen hostile to the position of the local bishop, Msgr. Bagnard, February 8, 1998, at Notre-Dame de Seillon (Péronnas, in l'Ain, France).

31. September 1999.

32. June 1998.

33. In the issue cited of *Documents Épiscopat*, Fr. Gagey expressed his disagreement with Fr. Moingt, but in a measured way: "Whoever lives out such a measure (non-sacramental in the narrow sense) has really made the intimate discovery of the grace of God spread by the Gospel and the life of the Church [...] It is one thing to experience the God who forgives, in the mediation of Scripture, fraternal prayer, the help of the Eucharist and spiritual aids, it is another to hear from the minister who has heard one confess his sin, 'Your sins are forgiven.'"

34. *Un christianisme d'avenir. Pour une nouvelle alliance entre raison et foi (A Christianity for the Future. For a New Alliance Between Reason and Faith)*, Seuil, 1999, p. 215.

35. In terms that are almost comical in their disproportion: *Ad Tuendam Fidem*: "The Church finds itself enclosed in a corset that could recall the worst moments of the pontificate of Pius XII," warned Henri Tincq in *Le Monde* on August 5, 1998; *Apostolos Suos* "muzzling the bishops," headlined the *National Catholic Reporter* of August 14, 1998; etc.

36. *La Documentation catholique*, August 4, 1991, p. 757.

37. *La Documentation catholique*, July 19, 1998, pp. 653-656.

38. *Code of Canon Law*, can. 749 § 3.

39. Commentary on *Ad Tuendam Fidem*, n. 9.

40. Commentary on *Ad Tuendam Fidem*, nn. 9 and 11 § 4.

41. L'Age d'Homme, 1998.

42. Cardinal Martini had already said clearly that one could renounce the Latin discipline of ecclesiastical celibacy "as an exception, in the face of certain situations" (interview in *Le Monde*, January 4, 1994).

43. The same Cardinal Martini, in order to show that the Letter *Ordinatio Sacerdotalis* had not closed the debate, had explained that it did not exclude a feminine diaconate (*Adista*, June 11, 1994).

44. Among others, in a collection of interviews (*Nel cuore della Chiesa e del mondo* [*In the Heart of the Church and the World*], Marietti, Milan, 1991), the Archbishop of Milan, then candidate for cardinal, had declared that he disagreed with a "rabbinical" moralism, and that he preferred by far a more positive preaching, more in line with the doctrine of St. Paul.

45. "The urban Christianity of today must assume an elevated historical role: to create a common fabric of values upon which may rest differences that are no longer devastating." (*"Il seme, Il lievito e il piccolo gregge"*, the seed, the leaven and the little flock, *La Civiltà Cattolica*, January 2, 1999, p. 10.)

46. *Op. cit.*

47. "There is a high degree of possibility that the next conclave will be a referendum for or against Martini. For or against a new council. For or against a reform of the papacy." (Henri Tincq, *Le Monde*, October 27, 1999.)

48. "The proposal of Martini goes far beyond suggesting a council for the next decade" (Joaquim Gomis, *El Ciervo*, Barcelona, November 1999.)

49. December 9, 1999.

50. January 9, 2000.

51. Under this working hypothesis, episcopal conferences could themselves be integrated into a framework of more extensive assemblies, representing opinion and venues for dialogue and discussion. In this regard note the meeting designated "Dialogue for Austria," convoked in Salzburg in October 1998 and presided over by Cardinal Christoph Schönborn, Archbishop of Vienna, and bringing together three hundred delegates from various dioceses. This synodal meeting at the level of the Austrian Church, in which were represented with particular prominence the most "progressive" tendencies, such as the movement "We are the Church," is the prototype of similar institutionalized meetings (it approved by now habitual resolutions calling for women deacons, the ordination of married men, the liberty of conscience for couples regarding contraception, the participation of local churches in the nomination of bishops).

52. January 2000.

53. *The Reform of the Papacy. The Costly Call to Christian Unity* (Crossroad, New York, 1999).

54. *Un christianisme d'avenir (A Christianity of the Future), op. cit.*, p. 205.

55. Letter to the Symposium for the Umpteenth Celebration of Vatican II, *Zenit*, March 1, 2000.

56. *Zenit*, March 1, 2000.

57. December 10, 1999.

58. At the moment I am writing, although these things mutate like clouds in the sky, the archetype of candidates of this "compromiser" tendency is the very wise Cardinal Bergoglio, Archbishop of Buenos Aires, conservative with broad ideas.

59. *La Documentation catholique*, March 17, 1996, pp. 251-266.

60. Cardinal Castrillón, Prefect of the Congregation for the Clergy, had discreetly met with a certain number of young French priests at Cluny on September 13, 1998, to allow them, over the heads of the French bishops, to express their grievances against the "dictatorship" of their elders and of the lay "soviets." It is reasonable that the "new bishops" in line with these priests and seminarians of the new type, these members of young congregations, are going to exploit the situation of "ideological weakness" — specifically, the foundering of the "post-conciliar" dreams — in order to exercise the greatest possible freedom of maneuver.

61. See notably the repeated attacks against the missal of Paul VI, in the monthly associated with *Comunione e Liberazione*, especially from the pen of Lorenzo Bianchi (for example, in the issue of January 2003, a study on the "silences" of the "reformed missal" concerning the Judgment and hell).

62. *Christus Dominus*, n. 6

63. *Humanae*, n. 7. "The usages of society are to be the usages of freedom in their full range: that is, the freedom of man is to be respected as far as possible and is not to be curtailed except when and insofar as necessary," *Dignitatis Humanae*, n. 7.

64. "The passionate interest of the diocesan Synods," wrote Monique Hébrard in the preface of *Révolution tranquille chez les catholiques. Voyage au pays des Synodes diocésains (Tranquil Revolution Among Catholics. Voyage to the Country of the Diocesan Synods*, Centurion, 1989), "is that they are a proving ground for truth between the mentalities and functioning, theology and ecclesiology which are vestiges of Vatican I, on the one hand, and on the other, the reality of Christian communities and challenges of the contemporary world which call for a creative reception of Vatican II." See also a specialist of this type of reflection, Jean Rigal, *Préparer l'avenir de l'Eglise (Preparing the Future of the Church)*, Cerf, 1990.

65. See in this regard the colloquium that was held in July 2001 at the abbey of Fontgombault, presided by Cardinal Ratzinger, and whose acts were published under the title *Autour de la question liturgique (Surrounding the Liturgical Question)*, *Association Petrus a Stella*, 36200 Fontgombault, 2001.

BIOGRAPHY

Claude Barthe, born in 1947, studied history at the University of Toulouse and obtained a Master's of Civil Law at the University of Paris-Assas. He later pursued ecclesiastic studies at the Catholic Institute of Toulouse and was ordained a priest of the Society of Saint Pius X in 1979. Having withdrawn from that society, Fr. Barthe possesses a *celebret* from the Holy See for celebrating the traditional Latin Mass.

In addition to the publications listed at the beginning of this volume, Fr. Barthe is religious reviewer for the quarterly *Catholica*. He also directs *Les cahiers du Roseau d'Or*, a journal devoted to the relations between novelists and Catholicism. He is the author of many articles and essays about the current crisis in the church.